INSIDE THE MINDS

Navigating Government Immigration Issues

Leading Immigration and Refugee Resettlement Experts on Addressing Employment, Education, and Health Care Issues for Immigrants

ASPATORE

Mat #40795790

BOOK & ARTICLE IDEA SUBMISSIONS

If you are a C-Level executive, senior lawyer, or venture capitalist interested in submitting a book or article idea to the Aspatore editorial board for review, please e-mail TLR.AspatoreAuthors@thomson.com. Aspatore is especially looking for highly specific ideas that would have a direct financial impact on behalf of a reader. Completed publications can range from 2 to 2,000 pages. Include your book/article idea, biography, and any additional pertinent information.

Inside the Minds Project Manager, Kristen Skarupa; edited by Eddie Fournier; proofread by

Material in this book is for educational purposes only. This book is sold with the understanding that neither any of the authors nor the publisher is engaged in rendering legal, accounting, investment, or any other professional service. Neither the publisher nor the authors assume any liability for any errors or omissions or for how this book or its contents are used or interpreted or for any consequences resulting directly or indirectly from the use of this book. For legal advice or any other, please consult your personal lawyer or the appropriate professional.

The views expressed by the individuals in this book (or the individuals on the cover) do not necessarily reflect the views shared by the companies they are employed by (or the companies mentioned in this book). The employment status and affiliations of authors with the companies referenced are subject to change.

Aspatore books may be purchased for educational, business, or sales promotional use. For information, please e-mail West.customer.service@thomson.com.

ISBN 978-0-314-19482-4

For corrections, updates, comments or any other inquiries please e-mail TLR.AspatoreEditorial@thomson.com.

First Printing, 2008
10 9 8 7 6 5 4 3 2 1

CONTENTS

Differentiating Between Refugees and Immigrants: Two Sets of Challenges

Caitriona Lyons

Refugee Program Coordinator

Texas Health and Human Services Commission

ASPATORE

Refugees and Immigration Policy

The U.S. immigration policy is a complex system of laws and regulatory framework, which is set at the federal level. The Department of Homeland Security, Department of State, Population, Refugee and Migration (PRM), Department of Health and Human Services, Office of Refugee Resettlement (ORR), Department of Justice (DOJ), and Department of Labor (DOL) are the primary U.S. federal agencies involved in immigration policy. Under the Department of Homeland Security, the U.S. Citizenship and Immigration Services (USCIS) is charged with implementing immigration admissions, while the Immigration Customs Enforcement (ICE) and Customs and Border Protection (CBP) divisions carry out the enforcement of immigration policy.

PRM coordinates U.S. international population policy and works closely with the U.S. Agency for International Development, which administers U.S. international population programs. The Bureau also coordinates U.S. international migration policy within the U.S. government. PRM also provides oversight of the admissions of refugees to the United States for permanent resettlement. ORR has oversight of federal funds to assist refugees resettled in the U.S. The Department of Labor (DOL) administers and enforces more than 180 federal laws. These mandates and the regulations that implement them cover many workplace activities. The DOJ's Office of Civil Rights provides services and protections for victims of trafficking—a modern day form of slavery—and provides guidance and laws regarding access to services for Limited English Proficient person. *See* www.state.gov/g/prm; www.usdoj.gov/whatwedo/whatwedo_ctip.htm; www.acfhhs.gov/programs/orr/policy/sl04-10.htm.

The Immigration and Nationality Act (INA) and its amendments are the basis for most immigration laws in the U.S. A legal permanent resident (LPR) or "green card" holder is defined as a person who has been granted lawful permanent residence in the U.S. In 2007, 1,052,415 persons became LPRs. Annual Flow Report, March 2008- Homeland Security.

U.S. law gives preferential immigration status to people with a close family relationship with a U.S. citizen or legal permanent resident, people with needed job skills, and people who qualify as refugees. Immigration is also limited for certain categories of immigrants, including family-sponsored preferences, employment-based preferences, and diversity immigrants. A per-country ceiling is also calculated each year. Some major categories, such as immediate relatives of U.S. citizens, are exempted from the per-country limit. Other categories of immigrants—for example, asylees and refugees—are also subject to numerical limitations. There are two paths to LPR status. Foreign nationals living abroad apply for an immigrant visa at a consular office of the Department of State; persons living in the U.S., who qualify for legal permanent residence, including refugees and asylees, file an application for adjustment of status to LPR with the USCIS. Most LPRs who are at least eighteen years of age and can meet other certain requirements are eligible for citizenship following five years of LPR status in the U.S. They must successfully pass an English language, civics, and history test. LPR children under eighteen years of age may acquire citizenship from their U.S. citizen parents (Annual Flow Report, March 2008, Homeland Security).

The Refugee Resettlement program enacted by Congress in 1980 is a small and distinct component of the system by which people can gain legal entry to the United States. Under the 1980 Refugee Act, the federal government guarantees assistance and services to refugees, based on the understanding that they have lost their country and belongings and are forced to flee due to fear of persecution due to their race, religion, nationality, membership in a particular social group, or political opinion. *See* The Refugee Act of 1980, Pub. L. No. 96-212, as amended by the Refugee Assistance Extension Act of 1986, Pub. L. No. 99-605, 8 U.S.C. § 1522(c); section 501(a) of the Refugee Education Assistance Act of 1980, Pub. L. No. 96-422, 8 U.S.C. § 1522, section 584(c) of the Foreign Operations, Export Financing and Related Appropriations Act, 1988, as included in the FFY 1988 Continuing Resolution, Pub. L. No. 1000-461 and 1991. Pub. L. No. 101-513.

Applicants for refugee admission to the United States must meet the following criteria:

1) Meet the definition of "refugee" contained in the U.S. Immigration and Nationality Act
2) Be among those refugees determined by the president to be of special humanitarian concern to the United States

3) Be otherwise admissible under U.S. law
4) Not be firmly resettled in any foreign country

The implementation of refugee policy is split between four federal agencies with broad areas of responsibility:

1) Department of State: Establishes policies concerning admissions and early resettlement services
2) Department of Homeland Security-U.S. Citizenship and Immigration Services: Provides legal adjudication and citizenship services
3) Department of Labor: Oversees labor migration issues
4) U.S. Department of Health and Human Services: Funds social service programs

Refugees are identified as needing a durable solution to resettle to a third country because they are unable to return to their home or integrate safely in the country of first asylum and are in need of protection and resettlement to a third country including the United States.

The number of refugees admitted each year is established by the president in consultation with Congress, the Department of State, certain non-governmental organizations, and the UNHCR. The president also sets national admissions and determines designated nationalities and processing priorities for the following year. Since 1975, the U.S. has resettled more than 2.6 million refugees with annual admissions ranging from 207,000 in 1980 to a low of 27,110 in 2002. Refugee Council USA- U.S. Refugee Admission Program for Fiscal Year 2006-2007, September 2006.

The cornerstone of refugee resettlement in the United States is family reunification. A priority system for admissions is used to process refugee applications. The majority of refugees arrive in the United States through the established overseas program with approved immigration status, while a smaller number obtain status through the domestic asylum process.

The objective of refugee assistance programs is to help refugees find jobs and adjust to life in the United States as soon as possible. This is accomplished through a public-private partnership that includes federal, state, and local government, and provides a significant role for private charitable groups, volunteers, and churches, and relies to a large extent on private contributions.

Funding for U.S. domestic refugee social service is received through two paths. The Department of State funds early reception and placement through a system of recognized refugee national Voluntary Agencies (VolAgs) that in turn fund local affiliates. The Department of Health and Human Services, Office of Refugee Resettlement (HHS-ORR) provides funding for longer-term resettlement services to national VolAgs, states, and local affiliates. In addition, many non-governmental agencies receive matching grant funding from HHS-ORR to provide alternative assistance to welfare assistance for refugees during the initial resettlement period.

Refugee populations are eligible for the same public benefits and services as are U.S. citizens. Refugees and asylees are eligible to adjust status to legal permanent resident after one year of residence in the United States and can apply for citizenship five years from their date of entry.

The state or authorized entity provides services after initial resettlement to help refugees become employed, learn English, and adjust to cultural differences. Effective June 15, 2000, asylees with approved petitions are also eligible for Refugee Cash Assistance and Medical Assistance as of the date of their approved application for a period of eight months, and as of May 2001, Victims of Severe Forms of Trafficking are eligible for benefits and services to the same extent as refugees.

The Thirteenth Amendment to the U.S. Constitution outlaws slavery and involuntary servitude. Traffickers force their victims into the international sex trade, prostitution, and forced slave labor through coercion, threats of physical violence, psychological abuse, torture, and imprisonment. To deter these crimes, Congress passed the Victims of Trafficking and Violence Protection Act (VTVPA) in October 2000. VTVPA provides resources to combat trafficking in persons and to provide services and protections for victims.

Under this law, the Office of Refugee Resettlement (ORR) of the U.S. Department of Health and Human Services (DHHS) is designated as the agency responsible for certifying that adult individuals meet the criteria. To receive a certification, ORR must determine if the adult individual has been subjected to a severe form of trafficking and whether the victim is willing to assist with the investigation and prosecution of trafficking cases and has made an application for a visa under section 101(a)(15)(T) of the Immigration and Nationality (INS) Act, or whose continued presence in the United States will ensure the attorney general of a trafficking prosecution. Upon certification, ORR will issue letters of certification for adult victims.

Children under eighteen years of age who have been subjected to a severe form of trafficking do not need to be certified to receive benefits. ORR will issue letters, similar to the adult certification letters, stating that the child is a victim.

When victims of trafficking are certified by ORR, they are eligible for Refugee Social Services and Refugee Cash and Medical Assistance (CMA) to the same extent as are other refugees.

Issues

The United States has historically taken in more than half of the refugee population; however, in the years right after September 11, 2001, the U.S. cut its contribution dramatically. which not only changed the landscape of refugee resettlement, but also created challenges for service providers.

An admission ceiling of 70,000 refugees was approved in FFY 2002. But, due to a temporary suspension in refugee arrivals following Sept. 11 and new overseas security measures, only 27,110 new refugees resettled in the United States at the end of September 2002. This was far below the 70,000 ceiling set for the fiscal year ending Sept. 30, and below the 53,000 refugees who had arrived in the United States during the same period a year earlier *See* United States Committee on Refugees- Refugee Reports 2002.

Meanwhile, thousands of refugees who were approved for resettlement in the United States prior to the events of September 11, 2001, remained at risk in camps, living in dangerous conditions, facing hunger, disease, rape, or being forced to return to the countries from which they fled.

In recent years, the number of refugees to the U.S. has steadily recovered; arrival levels prior to the events of 9/11, however, are still far below the overall average number admitted between 1980 and 2002 of 98,000. The U.S. refugee program has received excellent support from the administration to restore the program as evidenced by the 80 percent admissions increase in 2004 increasing from 28,422 in FY03 to 52,868 in FY 2004 and 53,813 in FY05. Refugee Council USA- Sept. 2006. However several pieces of legislation have been enacted and implemented to counter terrorism that have unintended consequences for refugees and other populations legally in the United States or applying for resettlement to the U.S. The bar to refugee admissions was greatly expanded by the USA Patriot Act of 2001 and the Real ID Act of 2005. The material support ground of inadmissibility has been applied to deny refugee status and protection to refugees and asylum seekers who have been coerced to provide material support—often under gunpoint—to groups of two or more persons deemed to be involved in "terrorist activity." The result in FY 06 was that despite a presidential determination authorizing 70,000 refugee admissions, only 31,912 refugees were authorized to enter the U.S. *Id.* The broad definition of terrorist activity also affects U.S. allies or groups that supported the U.S. The administration has recognized the need to address this issue and has provided waivers for certain groups of refugees that meet all other eligibility requirements for resettlement and do not pose a threat to the safety and security of the U.S. These efforts are very much appreciated; however, additional legislative remedies are needed to address the broad definition of the material support bar.

The Real ID Act of 2005 is a part of the Emergency Supplemental Appropriations Act for Defense, the global War on Terror, and Tsunami Relief, 2005. Title II, Section 202 of the Real ID Act mandates improved security for state issued driver's license and personal identification cards. The Act sets forth minimum issuance standards for verification of information presented, evidence that the person is in the U.S. lawfully, and issuance of temporary driver's licenses or ID cards to persons temporarily present in the U.S. The Act states (although several states have requested and been granted a deferment to implement until 2009) that only certain forms of documentation will be authorized to prove identity and eligibility for state identification.

The issue is that many refugees, asylees, Cuban/Haitian entrants, or Certified Victims of Trafficking may not possess the photo ID required for the license application. Many of these populations initially possess no photo ID due to the immediate and forced uprooting from their homes to seek protection and their first photo ID is the Employment Authorization Document (EAD). While this document would suffice for Real ID purposes as proof of lawful presence in the U.S., there can be delays of up to six months after arrival in processing, replacement, and renewal of EADs. This poses a quandary for refugee populations and the agency staff providing assistance because many programs are limited to the first four to eight months after arrival, during which time the refugees should be actively seeking employment and integration in their new communities. The lack of state identification can stand in the way of opening a bank account, signing a lease, or having utilities/phones started, and to some extent cause delays in finding employment because employers are reluctant to accept the I-94 document as sufficient proof of lawful residency. Refugees are not required to have an employment authorization document for employment but due to the recent crackdown by the enforcement arm of immigration, there is a lot of fear among employers that they will be fined unless they can show proof of the EAD. To some extent, the EAD is a passport to open doors and employment.

The United States Refugee Program views the issue of refugee health care as a priority. All refugees undergo an overseas Visa Medical Examination that looks for "excludable medical conditions." This could delay or prevent a person from traveling to the U.S. unless treated. However, the limited overseas exam is not a comprehensive physical exam and upon arrival, all refugees are referred for an enhanced domestic screening and assessment. Funding is provided to all states from the ORR for refugee health screenings and other preventative health programs. The basis for the refugee health screening programs is to provide services in a manner that is linguistically and culturally appropriate. Several programs also provide interpreter support for outreach and clinic services.

Many refugees have witnessed or were victims of torture and other lasting traumatic experiences prior to their arrival in the U.S. The immediate and long-term difficulties in adjusting to a new culture may compound stress and result in more serious mental health problems. Challenges to the program include how to address such issues during an initial screening and identifying culturally appropriate resources for any necessary referrals.

There are other special program eligible groups, such as asylees and victims of trafficking, who have not undergone the visa medical examination process overseas because their immigration adjustment occurs within the U.S., yet still exhibit many of the same health conditions as refugees. Special coordination with law enforcement, legal proceedings, and other support agencies are required for proper attention and handling of these clients.

Additionally, victims of trafficking, prior to ORR certification, are not eligible for refugee funded health services. This represents a major need and gap in needed services. The program is also challenged by the need for trained interpreters. Many refugees do not speak English well, or at all, and must rely on interpreters to convey their health concerns. The use of trained face-to-face interpreters is preferable as there are legal, moral (confidentiality), and ethical objections to using untrained family members, especially children, friends, people "off the street," as well as untrained bilingual staff. While trained interpreters in person are best, it can also be impractical or unavailable on short notice. Telephone interpreter services are an acceptable option, but may be costly.

The health care system in the U.S. is confusing enough for U.S. citizens, let alone for someone coming from another country who does not speak English or may have no experience with medical plans. Suddenly they are given six plans and asked to decide which is best for them. I have not heard any real discussions in my peer group about universal health care. Personally, I think it would be great for helping with immigrant needs.

Many employers now require English to work on their job sites, which presents a major barrier for refugee populations. Along with that, many job applications are now online. Some refugees are often not familiar with computers, let alone electricity, and may not know how to read or write in their own language, and certainly not in English. In these instances, refugee service providers rely on the close-working relationships they have fostered with area employers and have been able to work around this issue, but not in all cases. Certainly, we have found that many employers are very eager to have refugees employed in their company as they find that they are reliable, hardworking people.

In the economic downturn, it sometimes can be very difficult to hire someone who does not speak English and is not familiar with the Western culture. On the other hand, we are seeing a rising phenomenon resulting from recent immigration raids on large industries and manufacturing plants in which they are losing employees because they did not have legal immigration documentation. There seems to be a focus now on recruiting within refugee populations because they are here legally and on the path to citizenship. Certainly, refugees are free to move anywhere they want within the U.S., but the recruitment process for newly arrived refugees can be quite disrupting to the whole system of care. Newly arrived refugees are closely teamed with refugee resettlement agency staff and receiving orientation, language services and other services to help with their adjustment to the U.S. They are often also in the middle of medical treatments and vaccination series. Recruitment uproots them away to some remote area of the state, where there is no center to help them on their path to their integration and ultimately becoming U.S. citizens. The last thing we want to see is refugee populations exploited in any way. The potential is there for that to happen, unless we are able to talk to these companies and explain how refugees get here, why they come in, and the types of services they are going to need. Some of these jobs do pay well, and it is possibly a good position for refugees, but they do need other types of assistance beyond employment. This trend of refugee recruitment to industries and manufacturing plants has the potential to turn out as a positive development for refugee populations. We have been encouraged by the cooperation, and indeed, assistance with resources by some of these agencies to ensure a stable workforce and to provide accommodations for English language classes, transportation, and other services.

We have not run into too many obstacles within education with our refugee population. In Texas, as in many other states, legislation was passed to allow certain undocumented students to attend institutes of higher education at the state tuition rate. The requirements vary from state to state depending on length of residency and other factors such as graduation from an in-state high school.

The challenge for refugees coming from areas where there has been little or no formal education is placing them within a Western system. The second issue is how we communicate with these children, because they often speak dialects of languages that are not easily found.

However, there are several international schools that have been established and students placed in these schools for the first year or two after arriving in the U.S. tend to be successful. Going from there into regular schools and the whole testing environment is a big challenge for many of these children. Not that they are not trying, but rather learning a new language and system, a task that cannot always be accomplished within two years to be able to pass mandated state assessment tests. Refugee groups tend to value education highly so failure can be difficult for families and much pressure is placed on students to excel. An important program funded by the ORR through states is the refugee School Impact Program, which funds states to provide liaisons into the community to help bridge the cultural and language issues, and provide training in the schools about refugees.

Social programs and benefits like welfare used by U.S. citizens to access public benefits will also be used by refugees. There is temporary assistance for needy families, food stamps, and Medicaid. Some programs are funded on a time-limited basis for refugees. Some cash assistance programs and social services are specifically geared for refugees, to help them integrate into their community, such as ESL classes and driver's lessons. Numerous programs are available for refugees for a period of five years, and some are more limited, such as eight months for the cash assistance program.

Statistical use of public benefits indicates that refugee and immigrant population's use of public benefits is limited. Many refugee populations do not stay on public benefits for a long period of time. In Texas, the refugee use of temporary assistance for needy families is very low. Refugees come from so many different backgrounds, and most arriving from countries that did not have public benefit systems to begin with, so they have not participated in these types of programs before. Additionally, many refugees, similar to immigrant populations, have a strong work ethic and desire to move ahead. They often take two to three jobs to get by and avoid public assistance programs.

Another issue to consider, after education and public benefits, is that of law enforcement (LE) and the communication barrier. Many of these people come from a situation in which they feared law enforcement, so they are not going to turn to law enforcement for assistance if they get in trouble. LE staff may not be familiar with cultural aspects of refugee populations and often need an interpreter immediately to assess the situation. It is a difficult spot to be placed in—on the one hand needing to take prompt action and on the other, not fully understanding the complete picture. It goes both ways. Many of the refugee provider agencies work closely with local law enforcement and invite them to orientation sessions with newly arriving refugees. This has resulted in overcoming some barriers and raising awareness of available resources such as interpreters. Cross training is also occurring in the area of child protective services. Recent interaction with law enforcement has been very positive in the area of working with victims of trafficking. Across the country, social services, law enforcement, and health partners are truly partnering to provide services for those victims, and recognizing that it is absolutely essential to have all of those people at the table to be able to provide the services that are needed. That has been a good development over the past four to five years.

Legal and Political Aspects

Resettlement agencies provide orientation to newly arriving groups, and orientation definitely includes the laws of the land. This is a very important piece of the information that they receive when they arrive. It is provided to them continuously over a period of time so they will have some understanding of how our legal systems work. Refugees and other populations can adjust their status to legal permanent residency, and should do so after one year in the country. The legal issues for refugees and those of us assisting them include making sure that they have their work authorization and apply for their legal permanent residency after one year in the country. One problem is that there is very little funding to assist with the sometimes prohibitive costs of these adjustments. I am curious as to how the new fee increases for naturalization will play out. We have a large group of Somalian refugees who will be eligible to apply for citizenship next year. They tend to have large extended families, and given the cost of applying for citizenship, not all family members may be able to naturalize at the same time.

State regulations regarding refugees and immigrant assistance differs between states. The decentralization of the welfare system means if someone moves from one state to the next, the same services may not be available in the same manner. This difference can cause a lot of confusion initially. We have had some minors that have come from other states, and we have been able to get them into services. There has been a lot of cooperation and coordination across state lines, always keeping in mind the most important thing being the welfare of the child.

I cannot think of any agency that would not be to some extent impacted by or working with refugee and immigrant populations, the education agencies, and the workforce agencies. The Agencies on Aging also have come into contact with a lot of these individuals, along with legal services, law enforcement, whole city infrastructure, and a lot of the community agencies as well. There are some functions that only a U.S. citizen can participate in, such as voting or sitting on a jury.

All the U.S. refugee resettlement programs are actually part of the national system—ten national organizations and nine national resettlement programs. They have affiliate programs within each state. Those programs are very much involved and we have frequent interaction with those organizations. The National Law Center, the National Immigration Forum, and the CLINIC are very much a part of the system of providing advocacy and services for immigrants and for refugee populations.

Naturally, we are concerned about proposed changes to federal immigration law. Questions on the EADs and on the material support issue are big topics. Also, we are in the last year of an administration, and it is debatable how quickly changes will occur in federal immigration law. We are grateful for the continued commitment of the United States in providing protection and assistance to refugees. The U.S. refugee program is a time-honored tradition of opening our land and its opportunities to those among us who are the most oppressed and vulnerable in the world.

There is also no doubt that today's refugee world presents new challenges and a call for a new vision and recommendations for improvement and new approaches.

Refugee work is very complex and no single organization can possibly master all of its disciplines. The partnership between public and private entities is key to the development of the program in this more complex era.

I believe it is important to always remember that the refugee is ultimately making the changes in their life, and as such, their voice must be heard. We provide the information and perhaps some guidance, but ultimately we must have respect for those individuals and walk with them on their journey. Hope with them, encourage them to move forward, and believe in them. Refugees have changed my life with their strength, courage, and perseverance in overcoming enormous odds. Certainly some of these individuals have been the most resilient and extraordinary people I have ever encountered.

Caitriona Lyons, a native of Ireland, began her work in the area of refugee and immigration programs many years ago and is privileged to be working for the U.S. refugee program. She is currently the refugee program coordinator for the State of Texas, Health and Human Services Commission. Prior to this, she worked in the government relations department within the Texas Department of Human Services as an immigration specialist. She has extensive work experience in the nonprofit sector, including the direction of a refugee resettlement program in Austin for USCCB.

Ms. Lyons has a master's in human services administration from St. Edward's University and is a licensed social worker. She is currently serving on the State Bar of Texas Immigration Affairs committee and is on the Board for the Institute for Social and Economic Development. She served in the capacity of secretary for SCORR for two terms before being elected to the office of president for the State Coordinator's of Refugee Resettlement association in 2004. In June 2006, Ms. Lyons was awarded Outstanding American by Choice by the U.S. Citizenship and Immigration Services for her work with immigrants and refugees in Texas.

Dedication: *Dedicated to all of those involved with providing assistance for refugees and to the strength and courage of refugees worldwide.*

The History and Functions of the Office of Special Counsel for Immigration-Related Employment Discrimination

Patrick Shen

Former Special Counsel

U.S. Dept of Justice, Civil Rights Division, Office of Special Counsel for Immigration-Related Unfair Employment Practices

ASPATORE

Introduction

The Office of Special Counsel for Immigration-Related Unfair Employment Practices (OSC), a component of the Justice Department's Civil Rights Division, was created through the Immigration Reform and Control Act of 1986 (IRCA).[1] By imposing penalties on *employers* for hiring unauthorized workers, IRCA introduced a new approach to immigration policy during an era of heightened national concern over immigration issues.[2] OSC's mission was to enforce IRCA's new anti-discrimination provisions to be codified in the Immigration and Nationality Act (INA), providing an important counterbalance to newly introduced employer sanction laws.[3]

Prior to 1986, under federal immigration laws, only undocumented workers were liable for any penalties for unauthorized work.[4] Employers had no legal liability for hiring undocumented workers.[5] Among the many new requirements stemming from IRCA was the employer's duty to verify the work eligibility of new employees.[6] Specifically, after being hired, an employee must present documentation as proof of identity and employment eligibility to the employer, who then is required to verify the authenticity of the documentation and record this information on Form I-9.[7] The duty of an employer is only to make a good-faith determination as to whether the documentation appears genuine on its face and relates to the employee.[8]

Because of this new verification requirement, some members of Congress were concerned that employers might deny jobs to legal workers who

---

[1] Immigration Reform and Control Act of 1986, Pub. L. No. 99-603, 100 Stat. 3359 (Nov. 6, 1986) (partially codified in scattered sections of 8 U.S.C.).
[2] *See, e.g.*, Pear, Robert, *Close Vote Tense: Landmark Measure Goes to a Conference with Senate Members*, N.Y. Times, June 21, 1984, at A1; Bhagwati, Jagdish, Editorial, *Control Immigration at the Border*, Wall St. J., February 1, 1985, at 22 (for examples of national concern over immigration issues around the time of IRCA's passage).
[3] 8 U.S.C. § 1324b.
[4] Immigration and Nationality Act of 1952, Pub. L. No. 82- 414, 66 Stat. 163 (1952) (codified as amended at 8 U.S.C. §§ 1101- 1524).
[5] *Id.*
[6] 8 U.S.C. § 1324a(b).
[7] *Id.*
[8] 8 U.S.C. § 1324a(b)(1)(A)(ii).

looked or sounded "foreign" for fear (or purported fear) of inadvertently hiring unauthorized workers.[9] Representative Augustus Freeman Hawkins (D-CA) stated that, "bigotry and discrimination are alive and well in America ... And despite the laudable purpose behind this bill, there are those in this Nation who would use this measure as a pretext to deny employment to U.S. citizens and aliens lawfully residing here and by right, simply because they look or sound foreign."[10] Because of these misgivings about possible unintended consequences of the new requirements, Congress added an amendment to IRCA prohibiting discriminatory employment practices based upon citizenship status or national origin, as well as prohibiting the practice of over-documentation or "document abuse."[11] That same amendment created OSC to enforce these anti-discrimination provisions.[12] These concerns were substantiated in a Government Accounting Office (now the Government Accountability Office)(GAO) study in 1990, in which the GAO reported that, while it was difficult to determine whether discrimination was a direct result of IRCA, about 10 percent of employers began one or more discriminatory practices because of the changes to the law.[13] The study also found that persons of Hispanic and Asian origin suffered higher levels of discrimination, and that about 9 percent of employers said that they only hired U.S.-born persons, or did not hire persons with temporary work eligibility documents.[14]

More than twenty years later, as we face another wave of public anxiety about immigration enforcement and policy, OSC continues to play an important role alongside the Department of Homeland Security (DHS) in balancing the dual goals of establishing that all workers are authorized for employment, and protecting lawful workers from discrimination.

---

[9] 130 Cong. Rec., 15882 (1984), statement of Rep. William Blaine Richardson (D-NM): "[An] employer would not want to take a chance on hiring me because I am Hispanic and dark complexioned. The burden of proof would be on me to certify that I am a real American citizen with an identity card. This is how discrimination works. The perception would weigh against Americans of Hispanic origin that are not fair haired."

[10] 130 Cong. Rec., 15910 (1984), statement of Representative Augustus Freeman Hawkins (D-Calif.).

[11] 8 U.S.C. § 1324b.

[12] 8 U.S.C. § 1324b(c).

[13] U.S. General Accounting Office, *Immigration Reform: Employer Sanctions and the Question of Discrimination*, Report to the Congress, GAO/GGD-90-62, March 1990, p. 48.

[14] *Id.*

OSC Functions and Jurisdiction

The anti-discriminatory provisions of INA protect U.S. citizens and certain work-authorized individuals from employment discrimination based upon citizenship status or national origin.[15] The law also protects all work-authorized individuals from discriminatory documentary practices relating to the employment eligibility verification process, and from retaliation against those who take action against employers who discriminate.[16]

Prohibited Practices

Four types of conduct constitute prohibited unfair immigration-related employment practices under IRCA: citizenship status discrimination, national origin discrimination, document abuse, and retaliation.[17] OSC has jurisdiction over these four types of unlawful conduct.[18]

1. Citizenship Status Discrimination

The law prohibits discrimination based on citizenship or immigration status with respect to hiring, firing, and recruitment or referral for a fee by employers with four or more employees.[19] The law specifically protects U.S. citizens, recent permanent residents who applied for citizenship within six months of eligibility, temporary residents, asylees, and refugees.[20]

This means that, unless mandated by law or federal contract, employers may not limit hiring to U.S. citizens or any particular immigration status, so long as the job applicants are authorized to work in the United States.[21] Language such as "U.S. Citizens only" or "H-1B only" may be discriminatory on its face, and would constitute a violation of the law.[22] Moreover, OSC has consistently treated preference for undocumented

---

[15] 8 U.S.C. § 1324b(a)(1).
[16] 8 U.S.C. § 1324b(5)-(6).
[17] 8 U.S.C. § 1324b; 28 C.F.R. § 44.200.
[18] 8 U.S.C. § 1324b(c).
[19] 8 U.S.C. § 1324b(a)(1)(B).
[20] 8 U.S.C. § 1324b(a)(3).
[21] 8 U.S.C. § 1324b(a)(2)(C).
[22] *Id.*

workers over legal U.S. workers to be a violation of citizenship status discrimination as well as a violation of immigration laws.[23]

2. National Origin Discrimination

The law also prohibits national origin discrimination with respect to hiring, firing, and recruitment or referral for a fee by employers with between four and fourteen employees.[24] Specifically, employers may not treat individuals differently because of their place of birth, country of origin, ancestry, native language, accent or because they are perceived as looking or sounding "foreign."[25] IRCA's additional provisions prohibiting national origin discrimination serve as a complement to the previously existing Title VII protections, ensuring that all work-authorized individuals are afforded equal protection from discrimination.[26]

Under Title VII of the Civil Rights Act of 1964, the U.S. Equal Employment Opportunity Commission (EEOC) has jurisdiction over larger employers that commit national origin discrimination.[27] A Memorandum of Understanding between OSC and EEOC provides that the agencies shall refer any charges to the other that appear to fall under the other's jurisdiction, and that charges filed with one agency will be considered equivalent to having filed with the other for purposes of satisfying the statutory time limits. [28]

---

[23] *See, e.g., Iron Workers Local 455, et al. v. Lake Construction & Development Corp.*, 7 OCAHO No. 964, 1997 WL 1122231, 53 (September 12, 1997) (finding that Respondent had engaged in discrimination on the basis of citizenship status by preferring to employ an undocumented alien over qualified U.S. citizens).

[24] 8 U.S.C. § 1324b(a)(1)(A).

[25] *See Kanaji v. Children's Hosp. of Philadelphia*, 276 F.Supp.2d 399, 403 (E.D.Pa., 2003) (noting that "[i]n order to have a claim of national origin discrimination under Title VII, it is not necessary to show that the alleged discriminator knew the particular national origin group to which the complainant belonged . . . [I]t is enough to show that the complainant was treated differently because of his or her foreign accent, appearance or physical characteristics.").

[26] 8 U.S.C. § 1324b(a)(1)(A); *See also, Corneliu Curuta v. U.S. Water Conservation Lab*, 3 OCAHO No. 459, 1992 WL 535615, 1 (September 24, 1992) (noting that "[t]he legislative history of IRCA makes clear that the new prohibitions against national origin and citizenship status discrimination were enacted because Title VII remedies were considered insufficient.").

[27] 42 U.S.C. § 2000e.

[28] Office of Special Counsel for Immigration-Related Unfair Employment Practices; Coordination of Functions; Memorandum of Understanding, 63 Fed. Reg. 5518, 5519 (Feb. 3, 1998) (describing procedures for the referral of charges and the appointment of respective agents for the purpose of allowing charging parties to satisfy statutory time limits).

3. Document Abuse

During the employment eligibility verification Form I-9 process, an employer may not demand additional or different documents as evidence of an employee's identity and employment eligibility if the documents that the employee presents appear to be reasonably genuine on their face and relate to that employee.[29] The employee is only required to present documents that are deemed acceptable by the government and listed in Form I-9's instructions.[30] The employee must be given the choice of which documents to provide, and the employer should avoid asking for specific documents or requesting any additional documents if those provided are sufficient to establish identity and employment authorization.[31] An employer who knowingly and intentionally treats workers differently during the I-9 process, because of actual or perceived national origin or citizenship status, such as on the basis of an accent or "foreign" appearance, is committing document abuse in violation of federal law.[32]

A 1996 amendment to the statute, and subsequent case law, has established that document abuse is not a per se violation, but must be coupled with discriminatory intent.[33] The current statute states that the refusal of documents or request for additional documents violates the law "if made for the purpose or with the intent of discriminating against an individual."[34] A 2003 case emphasizes that "[i]f there is one thing that is crystal clear from the amending language, it is that document abuse can no longer be treated as a strict liability offense. While pre-amendment cases may have held that a showing of discrimination is not required in order to establish liability for document abuse, this principle no longer applies."[35]

---

[29] 8 U.S.C. § 1324b(a)(6).
[30] 8 U.S.C. § 1324a(b)(1)(A)(ii).
[31] *See United States of America v. Diversified Technology & Service of Virginia, Inc.*, 9 OCAHO No. 1095, 2003 WL 21130616, 22 (April 15, 2003) (stating that "the choice of which documents to present should be the employee's choice, not the employer's.").
[32] 8 U.S.C. § 1324b(a)(6).
[33] *Id.*; *See also*, *Diversified Technology*, WL 21130616, 14 (April 15, 2003) (holding that document abuse was no longer a strict liability offense).
[34] 8 U.S.C. § 1324b(a)(6).
[35] *Diversified Technology*, WL 21130616, 14 (April 15, 2003).

4. Retaliation

Finally, the law prohibits any intimidation, threats, coercion or retaliation of any kind against a person who intends to file or has filed an OSC charge or complaint, or testified, assisted or participated in an OSC investigation or proceeding.[36] This provision is "designed to protect any individual – that is, not just an employee, and not just a 'protected individual' under § 1324b ... from intimidation, coercion, or retaliation because the person participated in any manner in an investigation or proceeding under § 1324b."[37] The anti-retaliatory provisions play an important role in maintaining the integrity and effectiveness of OSC investigations by ensuring that individuals are not threatened or punished for providing information to OSC. A strict interpretation of this prohibition would include undocumented workers among the class of persons who have standing to bring a retaliation charge against an employer. However, since it is impossible for undocumented workers to claim relief such as back pay or reinstatement, OSC rarely receives charges from undocumented workers alleging retaliation.[38]

Filing Charges With OSC

Workers, or persons filing on their behalf, must file charges with OSC within 180 days of the alleged act of discrimination.[39] Charges may be filed in any language as OSC has the capacity to translate them into English. Once a charge is filed, OSC will investigate the claim.[40]

Typically, an attorney or investigator will interview injured parties, employers, and witnesses, as well as review documents.[41] After 120 days from receipt of the charge, if OSC is unable to make a determination, or dismisses the charge, OSC will notify the parties.[42] At that point, the charging party may file his own complaint before an administrative law

---

[36] 8 U.S.C. § 1324b(a)(5).
[37] *United States of America v. Hotel Martha Washington Corporation*, 6 OCAHO No. 846, 1996 WL 280768, 4 (March 15, 1996).
[38] *See, e.g.*, *Hoffman Plastic Compounds Inc. v N.L.R.B*, 535 U.S. 137, 138 (U.S., 2002) (holding that undocumented workers are ineligible for back pay).
[39] 8 U.S.C. § 1324b(d)(3); 28 CFR § 44.200.
[40] 8 U.S.C. § 1324b(d)(1).
[41] 28 CFR § 44.302.
[42] 8 U.S.C. § 1324b(d)(1); 28 CFR § 44.303.

judge.[43] The charging party must file his complaint within the following ninety days.[44] Where OSC has not yet made a determination regarding the charge, it may continue to investigate during this additional ninety-day period, and, where it finds reasonable cause to believe discrimination occurred, may also file a complaint against the employer before the administrative law judge, or seek to intervene in a complaint filed by the charging party.[45]

In the event that an aggrieved worker is not certain whether to file the complaint with OSC or EEOC, the worker may file a complaint with either OSC or EEOC, and the agency with the appropriate jurisdiction (sometimes both agencies) will handle the matter.[46]

Remedies

There are a number of remedies that may result from an investigation pursuant to 8 U.S.C. § 1324b. Injured parties may receive back pay for wages lost due to discrimination, and may also receive reinstatement or hire to a position.[47] Violating employers may be subject to civil penalties, which will increase in amount for repeat offenders.[48] OSC may also seek injunctive relief to end discriminatory practices and ensure that employers comply with anti-discriminatory regulations in the future. For example, OSC has enjoined successfully the placement of job postings that seek only workers with a particular visa status. In other instances, OSC has been able to require corporate human resources departments to conduct in-house training and institute best practices to avoid discrimination in the future.[49]

OSC's Successes

[43] 8 U.S.C. § 1324b(d)(2); 28 CFR § 44.303(c).
[44] *Id.*
[45] 28 CFR § 44.303(d)-(e) (stating that "The Special Counsel may seek to intervene at any time in any proceeding brought by a charging party before an administrative law judge.").
[46] Memorandum of Understanding, 63 Fed. Reg. 5518, 5519 (Feb. 3, 1998) (describing how EEOC and OSC may refer charges to one another).
[47] 8 U.S.C. § 1324b(g)(2)(B); *See also, e.g., Jones v. De Witt Nursing Home*, 1 OCAHO 189, 1990 WL 511979, 16 (June 29, 1990) (awarding back pay and restatement to employee terminated because of citizenship status).
[48] 8 U.S.C. § 1324b(g)(2)(B)(iv)(I)-(III).
[49] *See, e.g., Martinez v. Ray's Bar-B-Que*, 9 OCAHO 1120, 2005 WL 4911366, 5 (Dec. 19, 2005) (ordering that a violating employer comply with § 1324b and post notices advertising employees of their rights).

In FY2007, OSC successfully resolved almost 300 employment disputes. OSC considers a charge to be successfully resolved once a legal worker receives satisfactory compensation. Satisfactory compensation may consist of hiring or reinstatement to a job, full restoration of lost wages, or both. These successful resolutions occur through the settlement process, which means that the workers receive relief quickly and without the unnecessary delay of litigation.

Making Information Available to the Public

OSC prefers to educate employers and employees about their rights and obligations *before* violations occur, rather than to take remedial or punitive steps afterwards. For this reason, a significant part of OSC's mission is to make information available to the public, and to be a continuing resource to the members of the public who genuinely want to follow the law. Moreover, reducing instances of misunderstandings allows OSC to focus its enforcement resources on willful violators who intentionally discriminate against legal workers in the United States. Specifically, OSC has several ongoing programs to provide information to the public.

1. Public Education

OSC conducts an outreach and education program aimed at helping employers and employees understand their rights and obligations under the INA's anti-discrimination and employer sanction provisions. Each year, OSC awards grants to organizations across the country to conduct public education campaigns about OSC's mission and the anti-discrimination laws enacted through IRCA. The program is open to public service groups, faith-based organizations, associations, and other groups providing information services to employers and/or potential victims of immigration-related employment discrimination. In 2008, OSC awarded grants that ranged from $40,000 to $100,000 to eleven organizations serving communities throughout the United States. Additionally, OSC's staff has provided information in many public forums, such as seminars and conferences sponsored by public interest groups, trade associations, or educational institutions. OSC also tries to accommodate requests for speakers at events with fifty or more participants.

2. OSC Hotlines

Additionally, OSC operates employer and employee hotlines to address questions and resolve problems quickly. Each call is handled by either an attorney or an investigator. In FY2007, OSC received nearly 30,000 inquiries through the employer and employee hotlines. This "early intervention" program is a successful and cost-effective means of resolving workplace problems before employees file charges. Through the hotlines, OSC's staff resolves questions concerning proper employment eligibility verification procedures, and attempts to ensure that legal workers do not lose their jobs because of a misunderstanding of the law. Frequently, OSC staff is able to resolve potential immigration-related employment disputes within hours, rather than weeks or months, and without costly litigation. Employers benefit from the program because it saves them time and money. Workers benefit from it because it keeps them on the job.

3. Partnerships

OSC, in partnership with the EEOC, has participated in workshops for employers throughout the United States to increase understanding of employer sanctions and protections against discrimination. In addition, to increase accessibility to its services and resources OSC has signed and/or reinvigorated memoranda of understanding with numerous state and local human rights agencies, where individuals can now obtain information about OSC and file charges of immigration-related employment discrimination. These agreements permit individuals who file a timely charge of discrimination with an OSC memorandum-of-understanding partner to have their charge also considered by OSC, if it falls within OSC's jurisdiction.

Conclusion

As public awareness of worksite enforcement continues to grow, it is imperative that employers and employees alike understand and adhere to their rights and obligations under the anti-discrimination provisions of the INA. Employees who suspect that their legal right to work in the United States has been compromised because of discrimination, as well as employers who want to understand better their obligations under the law with respect to anti-discrimination provisions of IRCA, should call the OSC's hotlines for information or intervention. OSC will continue to utilize both enforcement measures and outreach education to ensure that all legal workers remain free from unlawful discrimination.

Patrick Shen was confirmed unanimously by the United States Senate on October 4, 2007 to be special counsel for Immigration-Related Unfair Employment Practices in the Justice Department's Civil Rights Division. Previous to this appointment, Mr. Shen was director of Government Relations at Fragomen, Del Rey, Bernsen & Loewy LLP. He began his legal career through the Attorney General's Honor Program, and has served in the Justice Department in the capacities of law clerk for the United States Immigration Court, Assistant District Counsel for the former Immigration and Naturalization Service's New York District, Special Assistant U.S. Attorney in the Eastern District of New York, and trial attorney in the Office of Immigration Litigation of the Civil Division. In addition, Mr. Shen was chief immigration counsel for the Senate Judiciary Committee during the 108th Congress, and director of Policy and Planning of U.S. Immigration and Customs Enforcement in the Homeland Security Department.

Prior to attending and graduating from Brigham Young University Law School, Mr. Shen was a sports reporter in Taiwan. He now resides with his wife and two children in Maryland, where he is a certified emergency medical technician and a volunteer with his local fire department.

Acknowledgment: *The author would like to thank Vanessa Reid, a Juris Doctor candidate at the University of California at Berkeley and an editor for the* Berkeley Journal of Gender, Law & Justice, *for her valuable contribution to this chapter.*

Note: *Author is writing in his personal capacity.*

Demand and Division: Immigration Law in Today's United States

José A. Olivieri

Partner

Michael Best & Friedrich

ASPATORE

Introduction

As an immigration attorney, my primary responsibility is to navigate the complex U.S. immigration laws in order to facilitate the movement of human resources across borders for my business clients. An issue rising in urgency and importance in immigration today is the growing need in the United States for college educated employees with technical talents in specific areas, including engineering, computer science, chemistry, biology, and related fields. Another driving need in the immigration field is on the opposite side of the employment spectrum, where employers seek to fill positions that do not require significant levels of education. These unskilled service positions could be easily filled by immigrant labor—if such can be secured legally.

Immigration and employment issues and problems are intensifying. Despite the occasional recession, the United States has experienced an almost continuous growth since the early 1980s, and the significant demand for workers in the two areas outlined above has increased. The problem faced is one of a supply-side breakdown. The United States demands workers, both superlatively skilled and unskilled, and our current atmosphere of recession notwithstanding, our supply of labor to fill these positions in demand is insufficient. Even if a decrease in demand may be taken as a given, accounting for an expected downward economic spiral in the United States, we are likely to still face issues of inadequate human resources supply in the future.

Most of the work that we do in my practice is in the service sectors, including information, systems consulting, financial services, and health care. We also act as counsel for colleges and universities. We do not handle many unskilled immigration cases. In the United States, we do not have a mechanism with which to bring in unskilled foreign nationals and this exacerbates the supply and demand problem mentioned above. Many of the unskilled positions that demand labor, thankfully, are assembly-line manufacturing positions, and since manufacturing is typically a higher-paying sector, its companies have had some success in sustaining some U.S. worker sources, creating less need to reach out to international labor markets.

Issues in Immigration Law, Recent Past to Present

Emerging Immigration Issues from the Past Year

Several immigration issues emerged in the past year, including an enhanced enforcement of United States immigration laws prohibiting the employment of people who do not have authorization to work in the country. A second major issue was the rising demand for professional employees in the face of the limiting factor of a finite—and insufficient—number of visas available under the H-1B category. In 2008, to obtain H-1B status for employees, company clients had to file on April 1, 2008 to obtain for the next fiscal year, and all of the available visas were used up in the first group of initial filings. The visa shortage necessitated significant forethought and planning, including contingency planning for the possibility that one's application was not picked in the lottery. This past year was also another year of a shortage in unskilled temporary labor in the H-2B category and another year of deepening problems with permanent resident applications stuck in the visa number pipeline. As with H-1B visas, there simply are not enough permanent resident visas available on an annual basis to meet demand.

Another significant issue last year was the United States government's expansion of the use of immigration systems like E-Verify. Our company clients are still learning about and trying to deal with E-Verify, which is a tool to help employers verify the work authorization of the employees, and which may also figure into enforcement strategy, though it is not specifically related to prosecution.

A final development from the past year in immigration law was the U.S. government's attempt to ease some of the discomfort created by the H-1B shortage by expanding the role of employment authorization for foreign students who have graduated from schools in the U.S.

In my practice, I encounter permanent residency visa problems primarily through my business clients. There are different categories that people fit into for the purposes of establishing permanent U.S. residency ("green card"). If a foreign worker seeks permanent residence through his or her employment, and the foreign worker has a job that requires, for example, a bachelor's degree and a couple of years of experience, then that foreign worker can expect a significant delay in gaining permanent residence due to the high demand for that kind of visa. The demand for the permanent residence visa, in the above example, outstrips the supply of visa numbers, and great delay and frustrations result. It could take years to receive final approval, even if everything has been correctly filed and documented.

The problems of the past year carry into the present and promise to continue in the future. As the economy changes, we will see a slowdown in hiring. This slowdown will affect employment demand issues at all levels, so the visa shortage problems might be somewhat mitigated as demand for employees decreases. Regarding enforcement, the conventional wisdom in immigration law is that when the country faces economic challenges, we are more likely to scrutinize our immigration policy and immigration enforcement in a push to eliminate competition for a shrinking pool of U.S. jobs by those who are not authorized to be in the country. Immigration issues promise to continue to be prominent on a local and federal level. While a decrease in petition activity may be detected, increases in enforcement activity will also occur.

Immigration Law in the U.S.: Political and Social Trends

Socioeconomically, the ascendance of the global marketplace and the opening of more markets worldwide have affected immigration, while the immigration law has not been adequately reformed to address the change in the marketplace. In the world today, free markets in terms of goods, services, and the flow of capital are easy to find, but immigration laws remain as significant obstacles to the lawful movement of human resources. The opening of the market and the rigidity of immigration laws has strongly influenced the large population of unauthorized workers in this country. People are following the flow of economic activity. As we become more global, instead of moving to the next city for work, people are increasingly moving to the next country or even continent. Socially, our aging population has also affected immigration, especially as it concerns the prospect of large-scale retirements and enrollments in social programs. Politically, Congress' attempts to address immigration reform have failed and each side of the debate is firmly entrenched into opposing positions, with a resulting stalemate. It has proven impossible to pass any manner of immigration legislation in the recent past, and there is little reason to expect decision-making parties to act in any more accord in the near future.

In terms of enforcement activity, whether they are criminal or civil investigations, audit and review activity has significantly increased in the last two years. Dating to 2002, there were very few prosecutions in the U.S. for the employment of unauthorized individuals; there are many more today.[1] Not only are the prosecutions on the increase, the nature of the prosecutions are increasing in variance. Today, we see more use of criminal law and criminal law tools, such as search warrants, surveillance tools, wire tapping, and other activities previously seldom employed in the immigration enforcement area.

Immigration Law Resources

A number of resources may be employed in tracking relevant trends in immigration law. The American Immigration of Laws Association (AILA), keeps its members informed of trends, and provides other excellent informational resources, including an array of daily publications dealing with immigration topics. AILA also effectively communicates the concerns, questions, and interests of immigrations lawyers in the United States to the Department of Homeland Security, the Department of Labor, and the State Department, which all have some role in immigration.

Immigration law is a fluid and evolving area that demands daily attention. Immigration law is influenced by a large amount of administrative guidance that is not necessarily in the form of regulation, but rather is communicated in the forms of responses to letters and of liaison meetings with the government. Immigration law guidance may be viewed as "informal," as opposed to the guidance easily found and digested in other areas of law, which takes the form of cases that might be reviewed or statutes and regulations that might be studied.

---

[1] U.S. Immigration and Customs Enforcement, Worksite Enforcement Fact Sheets (8/12/08), available at http://www.ice.gov/pi/news/factsheets/worksite.htm

Immigration Law and the Client

In my practice, we employ a recommended compliance checklist of steps relating to the Immigration Reform & Control Act of 1986, which prohibits the hiring of people who are not authorized to work in the United States, and further requires that all employers complete an I-9 form for all employees. The importance of the checklist has increased in step with the rising levels of enforcement activities, and some parts of the client checklist have changed as immigration laws have evolved. Today, for instance, we provide guidance for visits by immigration officers, including a list of documentation that should be in place and a plan to deal with that possibility. The stakes involved in immigration enforcement have increased; we no longer need to worry only about civil fines, but must instead be mindful of possible prosecutions and have detailed plans ready for the real threat of investigations.

Another recent change for the company client is the introduction of E-Verify. Employers that agree to participate in the computer-based E-Verify system and abide by its conditions can confirm the work authorization status of all new hires through the system. E-Verify compares the I-9 form information submitted by the employer against Social Security and Department of Homeland Security databases to determine whether the person is authorized to work in the United States. E-Verify is today being used by more than 60,000 employers in the United States. Although a significant number, it represents only a fraction of the total number of U.S. employers. Employers in the past never had to deal with anything like E-Verify. They never had to verify I-9 information with the government. Those who have enrolled in E-Verify to date have done so primarily on a volunteer basis. In certain situations, participation in E-Verify is required by law, but forced participation is limited and it is generally state-driven.

Issues in Immigration Law: A Look Ahead

One of the biggest problems with proposed reform of federal immigration rules is encountered in simply trying to enact the changes. The United States is a country divided on the issue of immigration. We have concerns about our substantial numbers of unauthorized workers and there is a resistance in Congress to passing legislation that might be viewed as a reward for people who have violated the law (i.e., unauthorized workers) or that may appear to be an incentive for more people to enter the country illegally in the future. Others believe that allowing even legal immigration to increase could have a detrimental impact on American workers. The divide may be, in part, geographical or demographical. For example, people from states that do not have a large foreign-born population may have less at stake politically. Conversely, the leaders who are likely to support some kind of immigration reform are from areas where there are significant foreign-born populations. If a senator hails from a state that does not have a significant foreign-born presence, and hears from other legislators concerned about the need to control borders and address security issues, he or she may not want to vote for a reform, given the dearth of political pressure from his or her voting population at home. Congressional breakdowns bear out the foreign-born populace divide for the last couple of votes on immigration reform issues; one can almost trace, state by state, the ethnic environments and match them to how representatives will vote on the reform. For an interesting attempt to analyze senator by senator the probability of reform see http://www4.uwm.edu/rhc/ about_us/publications.cfm, "An Analysis of the US Senate Debate and Vote on the Comprehensive Immigration Bill of 2007," presented by Enrique E. Figueroa, Ph.D., at the Roberto Hernandez Center Presentation, Milwaukee, WI, October 15, 2007.

It is not easy to enact any reform today, given our political environment. Even if we do manage to piece together and pass a reform bill, there are challenges and difficulties that seem almost insurmountable. A principle proposal of the last reform attempt was to change our permanent residence system entirely, such that it was no longer employer driven, but driven instead by a point system that would apply to each individual. Each person, in the proposed system, would have a number of points given to them based on characteristics such as education, age, etc., and they would gain entry into the United States through those characteristics, not based on an offer of a job, which is our current system. The proposed change would have been dramatic and would have had great potential for unforeseen consequences.

An H-1B increase is a necessary modification to immigration law. In addition, we must recapture many of the visa numbers that were not used in prior years. In some categories, there is not much demand. Since those visas were already approved, but unused, we may simply recapture them and use them to meet the demand in other areas, alleviating the incredible and frustrating delay we have been inflicting on people who have legally filed to stay here permanently. We must have a system in place that allows the U.S. government to know who enters the country and for what purpose. We do not have an effective system in place today. We do not have legal mechanisms for a large population of people who wish, with good intentions, to enter the United States, and as a result, many people use unlawful methods to gain entry.

Any time an immigration change comes along, we try to integrate that new feature into our timeline or checklist as soon as possible, often immediately, to avoid any consequences to a case for failing to implement the charge in a timely fashion. In communicating changes to clients, we employ a two-pronged approach. The micro approach keeps track of each case, its status, and ensures that the client is informed of status, case progress, and next steps. The macro approach prompts us to send out general alerts as different issues evolve, to write short articles for our newsletter on issues, to hold briefings for our clients, and to have annual conferences in order to educate and update our clients and prospective clients.

Generally, federal changes are much easier to keep track of because we know where the communication will come from and our national association keeps us informed. On the state level, effective and timely communication is more difficult to come by, and the multiple jurisdictions that might be involved in our practice further muddy the informational water. We consult informational Web sites, the entire functions of which are to track changes on, for example, E-Verify on a state-wide basis. For state legislation changes, the government relations part of our practice tracks bills, and we are told as soon as immigration related legislation is filed (though my practice's state—Wisconsin—has not been extremely active in the passage of these laws).

Concluding Advice for Immigration Attorneys and Other Practitioners

Immigration law is a demanding field that requires that its practitioners invest considerable time and resources in understanding and continuing to understand applicable law and the procedures. It is not a practice that may be dabbled in. Businesses should express their views to political leaders in the United States on the issue of immigration on an ongoing basis. Employers must plan, mindful of the movement of human resources throughout the world, because the complexity of immigration laws today requires forethought. Employers can no longer simply decide on a whim to hire whomever they wish—it takes planning. Finally, it is important that employers establish a compliance program to take into account all of the various U.S. immigration laws. Given the atmosphere of enhanced enforcement and divided immigration opinions in the country today, we must all be vocal, educated, continuously informed, and prepared.

José A. Olivieri is a partner in the Milwaukee office of Michael Best & Friedrich. He is the chair of the Employment Law Practice Group and founded the firm's Immigration Practice Group. Mr. Olivieri is listed in The Best Lawyers in America *and* Chambers USA. *He has extensive experience in the area of employment-based immigration matters, including B (temporary visitor), E (treaty trader/investor), F and M (student), H (temporary worker), J (exchange visitor), L (intracompany transferee), O and P (outstanding artist, scientist, educator, businessperson and/or athlete), R (religious worker), and TN (NAFTA) status, as well as permanent labor certification, national interest waiver, adjustment of status, consular processing, citizenship and naturalization and other immigration-related employment law matters, such as I-9 compliance.*

Mr. Olivieri also counsels management in other aspects of employment law such as matters of federal and state discrimination law; NLRB and WERC law; unemployment compensation; and labor contract administration.

He has taught the Advanced Employment Law Seminar at Marquette University Law School and is a frequent speaker on an array of immigration-related topics.

Integrating Immigrants to Build Stronger Communities

Richard Chacón

Executive Director

Massachusetts Office for Refugees and Immigrants

ASPATORE

Knowing our Newcomers

Since there often is not a clear understanding of the legal nuances between a refugee and an immigrant, misunderstandings of the differences between the two classifications can and do happen. Fortunately in Massachusetts, many institutions—such as clinics, hospitals, schools, and government agencies—have a better understanding of the differences between a refugee and an immigrant, and what that means for providing different kinds of benefits and services to help them.

There is still a need for a greater public education of the different kinds of categories that our newcomers fall into, and that is part of what we do here: reaching out to different organizations, constituencies, and communities to better educate them on the refugee population and the immigrant population, as well as the other groups, such as asylees and special immigrant visa groups here in Massachusetts. They are very different from each other, not just in terms of their status, but especially in terms of where they come from, what experiences they have had.

The kinds of benefits and protections given to refugees and asylees are substantively different—in terms of government-supplied cash assistance, job training, and English-language education—from those offered to legal immigrants. Legal immigrants are allowed to seek work and receive certain government services or benefits. The protections and benefits available for undocumented immigrants are far more limited. The complicated and increasingly fragmented national immigration system in this country has contributed to people's confusion over who can get what.

Our refugees tend to come largely from Africa and Asia, and now increasingly the Middle East, whereas our immigrants tend to come mostly from Latin America, Asia, and Europe. We do a lot of outreach to educate folks all across the state about our refugee and immigrant populations, what the distinctions are, and where they come from, just so they are aware of these people who are among us and that we walk by and deal with and interact with every day. Part of what I try to tell the public, whether through the media, or public hearings, or community outreach when I am asked to speak with different organizations, is reminding them just how much we are all interacting with each other. I love to cite the many different examples and figures of how much Massachusetts is already an immigrant and refugee community. A significant portion of the Boston Symphony is comprised of immigrants, and much of the faculty at MIT was born in another country. And perhaps the most revered institution here is the Boston Red Sox, a team formed increasingly of immigrants—players who were born outside of the U.S. Most of the Dunkin' Donuts franchises here and elsewhere are owned by immigrants. It is pervasive, and I try to remind people how it is already here.

When Governor Deval Patrick came into office, we as an administration were determined to find a better way to talk publicly about our immigrants and refugees, because we had noticed a toxic wave building, especially in other parts of the country where the talking about immigrants was more as threats and burdens. We want to change that conversation, so we recognize the assets and opportunities that our immigrants and refugees bring to the state.

Right now, immigrants make up 14 percent of the population in Massachusetts and 17 percent of the workforce. That percentage of the workforce has actually doubled over the last fifteen years. If not for these refugee and immigrant populations, Massachusetts would have seen a net decline in its population over the last several years. This is very important for us as a state as we approach the census in 2010, because our total population will help determine whether we are going to keep the current representation in Congress, and if we will continue to receive important grants and funds from the federal government that are sometimes based on population. The foreign-born population is extremely important for the future here in Massachusetts, so we need to be more educated about who they are and what we can do to better support them, so they can be productive and healthy members of our community.

The greatest challenge in working with both refugees and immigrants is making sure that they have the kinds of support and services they need to better integrate into their communities, the workforce, and the economy. By that, we mean things like improving their English skills, improving their educational levels, improving their job skills, so they can fill the employment gaps we have in our economy.

By extension, that leads to greater involvement in their communities, whether local government or civic groups, just getting them to vote and coming up with creative ways to get our refugees and immigrants better integrated into the communities. Another challenge is the question of status, particularly for immigrants. Our refugees already have legal status and protected status, but for a growing number of immigrants, the question of status continues to be the greatest challenge and the greatest priority.

Federal Immigration Reform and the States Push Toward Integration

Reforming the federal immigration process remains a challenge for our leaders—both executive and legislative—in Washington. We recognize that immigration law and enforcement has been and remains a responsibility for the federal government. But absent this reform, you are beginning to see a number of states come up with their own solutions to address the growing needs of immigrants and the communities where they are living, for example, through more programs to get immigrants to naturalize for U.S. Citizenship and more English-language classes.

I think there is still the hope that a new administration in Washington would be willing to address the obvious need for reform of the federal immigration laws, to help us get some clarity for those millions of people here in this country who need either legal status or a clearer path to citizenship. Secondly, I think there is a hope, or at least a question, of whether a new administration would change the emphasis in recent years on the heavy enforcement of deportations and enforcement raids that we have seen across the country. For a number of communities that has had a very big impact.

Many of us will be eager to see what a new administration will do with respect to policies on immigration and enforcement. Everybody is waiting to see what kind of leadership the new administration will bring in immigration policy and for refugee resettlement. These issues touch on so many different areas of federal government, whether the State Department, Department of Homeland Security, Department of Health and Human Services. Often the policies depend on the leadership in those agencies, so we are waiting to see what kind of leadership the new administration puts into these roles.

The movement of people, which we call migration or immigration, affects every facet of our society and our economy. Because of that, many people and organizations have opinions and responsibilities in determining how policies and programs get put into place. States are increasingly developing their own plans, based on the concept that immigrant integration should be the ultimate goal that best serves our newcomers and supports their larger community where they work and live.

A couple of years ago, Illinois started this process, developing an integration-based approach, heading up with policies and programs to help get people in these communities better integrated working with advocacy organizations, no-profit foundations, and business groups. We have a similar endeavor we started last summer that officially launched Massachusetts on an integration-based policy agenda, and that is what we are in the process of doing now.

In July 2008, Gov. Patrick signed Executive Order Number 503 that officially launched the "Massachusetts New Americans Agenda" initiative that will, through a series of public meetings across the state and close consultation with state agencies and immigration policy experts, develop a set of specific policy recommendation for how we as a state can better integrate our newcomers into the economy and for greater civic engagement.

Other states, such as Washington and Maryland, have followed the Illinois example. It is creating an emerging movement of states trying to be more proactive in how they address not only the needs of refugees and immigrants, but also the needs of local communities in helping them better understand these new arrivals and how they can address the impacts that these groups have brought. The great thing about this kind of initiative is that it brings together, in some cases for the first time, so many different individuals and constituencies to talk and work more collaboratively on developing a smarter approach to handling immigrant and refugee issues.

The Massachusetts New American's Agenda has brought together people from business, a governor's advisory council made up of academics, lawyers, health care professionals, immigrant entrepreneurs, people from the refugee service community, as well as from national and local foundations. We travel to different parts of the state to hear about their challenges and their accomplishments, and try to take all this input and develop a more coordinated and comprehensive plan that we are expected to present to the governor by July 2009. Immigration has such a wide effect and impact on a community and an economy, the only way to address it wisely is to bring in so many different groups. We are not always going to agree, but at least we are able to talk about it in a more productive way, in a more open way, to be able to come up with some solutions.

Employment, Health, and Education: Key Issues Facing Newcomers

The big issues in immigration and employment would first be in terms of making sure immigrants have the kind of documentation they will need to be able to apply for jobs or get work. Then, helping them understand what their rights are on the job, what kinds of protections they are entitled to; making sure they understand their basic human rights and their labor rights, so they are not prone to abuse. I think it involves making sure they have the kinds of language and vocational skills they need to be able to not just get a job, but to be able to move up their career ladder, so they can continue to advance in the economy and to their own self-sufficiency. I think it also means greater awareness of how to invest their money, how to save their money, and how to have access to credit.

We have some small programs that help refugees and immigrants who arrive with professional degrees or licenses get proper re-certification in their profession to continue working in their trade. We have seen the development of on-the-job English-language classes for refugee and immigrant workers. We have developed and supported programs that train refugees to work on farms and nurseries to help build the next generation of farmers. These examples are good starts, but there is a need for more training and education to help our immigrants attain the kinds of skills that we know they need in our present day economy.

Massachusetts is somewhat unique in that we have a new system in place that requires that everybody in the state have some form of health insurance. For those who cannot afford it, there are programs that help provide it. By and large, the biggest challenge is making people aware of what is out there to remove any confusion about the system in

Massachusetts. Then the next challenge is to try to encourage more families and individuals to understand the benefits of preventative health practices rather than waiting until you are sick, go for regular checkups or take your children for their checkups, or go to the dentist on a regular basis. Informing and encouraging preventative health is a major challenge for our new arrivals.

We have worked with our refugee populations to encourage them to get their health assessments; we try to educate them on the benefits of preventive western medicine to try to bridge any cultural gaps they have in their perspectives of health and medicine here from their home country. That's where culturally and linguistically appropriate training becomes so important. In Massachusetts, we have tried to expand the availability of professional translators and interpreters.

Sometimes we have to deal with issues related to cultural differences and approaches to health and medicine. In some cultures and communities, they have a different approach and attitude toward how to resolve health and medical issues. Often we have to try to bridge that gap and explain to them that they need not be fearful of a medical professional or of a particular instrument that the medical professional is using. A lot of cultural orientation goes into making sure that our refugees and immigrants get access to the kind of health care they need. Increasingly, we see the need for more culturally appropriate and linguistically appropriate mental health and emotional health services, particularly with a lot of our newer refugees. They are coming from places like Africa and Asia, where they have been living in refugee camps for five to ten years. They have not had access to traditional forms of health care or education, and many of them have suffered some level of trauma and continue to suffer some level of post-traumatic disorder. They are really in need of some mental health services. We also see an increasing need among our refugee and immigrant populations for greater understanding and awareness of laws involving sexual and domestic violence. Those are all key areas.

Refugees and asylees in Massachusetts are now given cultural orientation classes that include education and training on sexual and domestic violence laws and practices. We should do more for our immigrant communities, where we have seen a disproportionate number of abuse and violence cases.

In terms of education issues, the biggest challenge right now is the dropout rate, and how we keep our children, especially our immigrant children, in school. How do we keep them progressing? We have a great education system. This is where public education was born in America, and this continues to be a state that heavily emphasizes the importance of access to education. Governor Patrick recently announced a new vision for public education, which would provide a universal public education from pre-K to grade 14. We would move away from the old K-12 model, recognizing that there needs to be education earlier in life and longer, because of the way our economy is moving and that it is so service-oriented and requires so many additional skills. So keeping our children in school is the greatest challenge.

The second greatest challenge would be making sure that our youth—especially our refugee and immigrant children—have better access to the higher education they will need in order to succeed in the economy of today and tomorrow. The third challenge is adult education for our immigrants. That is increasingly a need we see everywhere in Massachusetts. There is a need across the state—and I would predict across many states—for adult basic education classes, especially among our immigrants. There is a waiting of 19,000 for ESL classes across Massachusetts. Having enough educational opportunities for our older adult immigrant population is very important.

Finally, I would say better access for childcare and early education opportunities for immigrant communities is important. As you and I know, in today's economy, families often have to have both parents working to make ends meet. We need to allow our immigrant communities and families better access to childcare and daycare services and early education slots, so both parents can have that opportunity to work. These refugees have been coming from refugee camps; they are learning for the first time how to use a stove or indoor plumbing, or how to make their way through a supermarket. These are all first-time experiences for them. It can be daunting for new immigrants to see snow for the first time.

We have begun working with our state agency responsible for early education and licensing for childcare to help them expand licensing opportunities for different immigrant and linguistic populations, but there is still a need for helping those communities get access to the kinds of funds they might need to meet licensing standards.

Legal Concerns

Along with helping immigrants and refugees acclimate to our economy and housing and education system, we see a need for better educating our new arrivals on the consequences of criminal activity. Families and individuals need to understand that if you commit a crime and you are convicted of that crime, you have no chance of staying in this country and obtaining citizenship, if that is eventually what you want. There needs to be better outreach and education to our different immigrant communities on the consequences of criminal activity, with the hope of discouraging more immigrants from getting involved in any kind of criminal activity.

Secondly, there needs to be better education for law enforcement organizations and individuals about different refugee and immigrant populations, who they are, where they come from, what it means to be a refugee versus an immigrant or asylee, and how to better communicate with these different populations. I think the greatest issue right now between refugees and immigrant populations and law enforcement is a lack of understanding and fear. Both contribute to what can be a very bad climate, both for the refugee and immigrant communities and for the police departments and the law enforcement authorities, who I believe really want to have positive relationships with their communities.

I have seen communities and police chiefs here in Massachusetts take a very collaborative and productive approach to communicating with different communities. I have seen how it leads to more effective strategies for community policing, relationships, and communications with leaders of different communities to have better approaches in place for that town or city. When this administration took office in January of 2007, one of the first things Governor Patrick did was to rescind a memorandum of understanding from the previous administration, between the Massachusetts State Police and the Federal Immigration Customs Enforcement Agency, allowing for some state troopers to be trained in federal immigration enforcement practices. The governor does not believe state law enforcement officials, or any state workers, should be in the business of enforcing federal immigration rules.

We get calls all the time from people trying to get legal status, or who are curious about how to get citizenship to be naturalized. First and foremost, legal assistance comes in the way of helping individuals or families get clarification on their own status. Secondly, I think we see the need for legal assistance in the area of policy, interpretation of federal or state laws and policies that would affect what we can provide as a state to different communities and different individuals. We work with immigration lawyers, and lawyers who are experts in asylum applications for individuals. Sometimes we refer people to these different lawyers who provide that kind of assistance. Then there are lawyers who are incredible resources as policy experts, immigration lawyers we have invited to help us work with different state agencies, to better understand their own policies and come up with better policies. These might be in terms of who might be eligible for certain kinds of services based on what kind of documentation they possess, whether it is a certain kind of visa, a certain kind of passport or employment authorization documents. There is a constant need for that kind of legal expertise.

Massachusetts has a vibrant network of immigration lawyers and firms that communicate regularly with us, such as the American Immigration Lawyers Association (AILA) or the Political Asylum/Immigrant Representation Project (PAIR). We also have a number of attorneys who offer pro bono services to refugees, asylees, and immigrant applicants.

To those who function in a role similar to mine in other states, I would say, first and foremost, you need to recognize that these new populations bring with them the very same hopes and dreams that the rest of us have. We want to have healthy, happy families, and lead productive lives. With that as your first basic understanding of these new populations, then you can start to understand how to better integrate and support these populations. We have always been at our best when we have embraced new communities and new arrivals and helped them get better integrated into American culture, American society, and American economy. As a state, try to develop as best you can a better coordinated plan for integrating these communities and populations into your communities and economies, because they are going to be the future of your state. You cannot just ignore a growing percentage of your population in the hopes that they are going to go away. That is a not a recipe for future success.

Look for ways to begin now to try to integrate these populations by bringing in many different voices from your state and your communities—whether it is in business, law enforcement, education, health care—to try to come up with the best answers that fit your particular state. Massachusetts is unique; we are not a border state with an international border, and we have a very different immigrant population. Unlike Texas, California, Florida, or Illinois, we are not dominated by any one group of national origin. For us, the challenges of addressing the needs of our immigrant populations are much more diverse. For the last seven years, most of our immigrants have come from Brazil, followed by China, so it is different. Because of all the colleges and universities we have here in Massachusetts, we have an immigrant population that is a rainbow of skills; everyone from a scientist down to a custodian, and they all contribute.

For people who do what I do in other states, trying hard to find ways to get their immigrant refugee populations to fill the gaps in their economies and integrating them is the best approach. Most of our immigrants are here legally, and they want to be better integrated. Discussions over immigration tend to go immediately to the undocumented immigrants, when in fact the majority of immigrants in this country are here with legal status. They want to be citizens, speak English well, get good jobs, and get great educations, just like the rest of us.

To prepare for the issues and changes yet to come, we must stay very closely connected to our representatives in Washington, to the members of our congressional delegation, about the trends and experiences that we have with our refugee and immigrant populations. We need to communicate with them what we need to see in any proposed federal immigration reform. I think we are fortunate in Massachusetts to have perhaps the wisest and most articulate voice on immigration in Senator Kennedy. He has been a tremendous leader on this issue, but other members of our delegation have also been incredibly knowledgeable and helpful on this. To the extent that our agency and this administration can continue in close communication with the members of our delegation on what we like or may not like in a particular proposal is extremely important for us, and not just us as a state.

The advocacy community and the business community need to be very clear and vocal about what we need and what we do not like. We have important relationships with different federal agencies and different people in those agencies who are setting policies or who could be a part of that discussion and those debates on whatever is proposed. Maintaining, and in some cases strengthening, our lines of communication with our representatives in Washington, in both the executive and legislative branch, will be one of our key roles in making our voice heard in whatever discussions emerge over immigration reform in the new administration.

Richard Chacón, executive director of the Massachusetts Office for Refugees and Immigrants, oversees the state agency that is chiefly responsible for the resettlement of refugees in Massachusetts and coordinates state policies and programs for the commonwealth's various immigrant communities. He was appointed in September 2007. Mr. Chacon previously served as director of policy for Massachusetts Governor Deval Patrick and as communications director for the Deval Patrick Committee.

Mr. Chacón worked for nearly two decades as a print and broadcast journalist including more than twelve years at the Boston Globe *in various reporting and editing positions, including Latin America bureau chief and deputy foreign affairs editor.*

In 2004, Mr. Chacón was awarded a Nieman Fellowship at Harvard University and this year was named an Eisenhower Fellow.

A native of El Paso, Texas, Mr. Chacón earned a bachelor's degree from Boston University, and holds master's degrees in public administration and journalism from Columbia University.

Partnership as the Key in Solving Immigration Issues

Edwin B. Silverman

Chief, Bureau of Refugee and Immigrant Services

Illinois Department of Human Services

ASPATORE

The Current Immigration Situation

As chief, Bureau of Refugee and Immigrant Services, Illinois Department of Human Services, the comprehensive array of immigration issues before us cross my desk, including those that affect refugees, asylees, parolees, victims of trafficking, legal permanent residents, unaccompanied alien minors, undocumented families, foreign visitors, and repatriates. Illinois has resettled 130,000 refugees and asylees since 1975. Over the past decade, we have averaged 40,000 new legal immigrants each year, and currently have 1.8 million foreign-born residents.

Needless to say, specialized legal assistance is required to address the needs of asylees (applicants with lawyers have a higher success rate), victims of trafficking, undocumented in detention deprived of legal counsel, unaccompanied alien minors in danger of inappropriate return to their home country, and those with temporary visas endeavoring to change status. Further, undocumented laborers are often exploited and deprived of labor rights. In Chicago, the National Center for Immigrant Justice has coordinated a network of hundreds of pro bono attorneys that has effectively addressed many of the issues we confront. Unfortunately, there are too many communities without such resources.

The Refugee Program is the nation's only immigrant program. Nationwide, we have provided up-front services—including English language training, adjustment counseling, health, mental health, and employment—to nearly 3 million refugees. The adults struggle in the process of adjustment, but make it, and the children flourish. A number of issues have affected the Refugee Resettlement efforts. From a legal perspective, the Department of Homeland Security has interpreted the "material support" clauses of The Patriot Act, Pub. L. No. 107-56, in an overly literal, restrictive manner, in effect casting many refugees in the same light as terrorists. The result has been a sharp reduction in refugee arrivals in the years 2002 to 2008.

The Refugee Program is per capita driven. The Reception and Placement grant to local refugee resettlement agencies is $430 per refugee arrival to establish the family household and sustain them for the first thirty days in the country. In 1975, the grant was $565 per arrival. If it were adjusted for inflation, it would be approximately $2,500 today. The agencies are responsible for rent, rent deposit, clothing, and furnishing the household with $430 per refugee. The Refugee Act of 1980 was established with the premise that refugees result from federal policy, and therefore the federal government is obligated to support the resettlement agencies, as well as state and local government. Beginning in 1987, the federal government has steadily diminished its commitment, at the same time that housing and other costs have continued to escalate. Without the generous support of the faith-based and other concerned communities, the Reception and Placement process would be unworkable.

Similarly, the Refugee Social Services allocation to states (based on the previous three years of arrivals) and the Targeted Assistance Grant to highly impacted counties (based on the previous five years of arrivals) have been based on flat congressional appropriations. In spite of the appropriation level, the federal government has added new categories of status to be served with these funds, including asylees, victims of trafficking, and foreign-born victims of domestic violence. Of late, refugee arrivals began to increase starting in July 2007. The funding to serve those increased numbers will not be available until September 2008. Moreover, refugee services are highly dependent on bilingual service delivery. Last year in Illinois, we served refugees with forty-seven languages. The increased caseloads per worker, and the lack of interpreter resources, have placed enormous stress on the resettlement system.

Labor and Legal Needs

Immigrant employment issues cut in several directions. With regard to low-income workers, there is inadequate staffing at the Department of Labor to conduct site reviews to uncover exploitation and abuse of employees. In addition, there is a built-in disincentive for undocumented immigrants to report abuse to the government, thus sustaining a corrupt system. With regard to well-educated immigrants, there are inadequate resources to enable re-certification of foreign-born professionals. The nation is losing billions of dollars in skilled labor while foreign-educated doctors, lawyers, and teachers are driving taxis. Further, the limitations on admission of H1b visas and others have prevented adequate numbers of new highly skilled workers from entering the labor force.

The failure of Congress to pass comprehensive immigration reform is appalling. As state-by-state data produced by the Migration Policy Institute demonstrates, the foreign-born percentage in the workforce exceeds their percentage of the total population. They are workers, sustainers of the Social security system, homeowners, and consumers. Further, there is no practical way to deport more than 12 million undocumented individuals. In the face of that reality, the Department of Homeland Security has turned to questionable tactics that split families, disrupt companies, and fundamentally erode American principles of human rights. It is an unfitting celebration of the sixtieth anniversary of the Universal Declaration of Human Rights, the articles of which speak to the right of movement between countries, to employment, to education, and to health care. Homeland Security's tactics feed racist, restrictionist propaganda by honing in on Mexican migration, when 40 percent or more of undocumented immigrants are visa over-stayers from Europe, Africa, and Asia rarely mentioned in the media.

When immigration reform is enacted, there will be a deep need for legal assistance. If there are, for argument's sake, 500,000 undocumented immigrants in Illinois, we will have to process almost 21,000 applications each month for two years. As we experienced with the Immigration Reform and Control Act of 1986, Pub.L. No. 99-603, which legalized 2.7 million undocumented immigrants nationwide, the role of attorneys in reviewing applications, resolving identity/name change, ensuring that clients with court histories do not jeopardize themselves, and covering other matters will be essential. Can a cost-effective process be put in place to meet the systemic needs? Further, as with the 1986 law, it is most certain that English language acquisition will be a requirement. If our 500,000 all need classes, and they were able to acquire certification in eight weeks, Illinois would add 4,200 students for each eight weeks for two years, and need 200 new teachers. Will Congress provide the resources? Can the state find the teachers? Can the state find the classrooms? All are serious challenges. For the legalization process begun in 1986, the federal government provided State Legalization Impact Assistance Grants, and Illinois was heavily dependent on community-based organizations to provide the language training. Finally, the 1986 law made it illegal for employers to hire out of status labor. However, Congress has never provided the resources for a reliable data system, whereby the work-eligibility of prospective employees could be verified. All in all, the legal, medical, and language training costs associated with legalization represent as great or greater a barrier as the nativist anti-immigrant sentiments that pervade some communities.

In contrast, the state of Illinois is a leader in providing welcome to new Americans. In addition to a holistic array of services for refugees, the Bureau administers an Outreach and Interpretation Program (thirty-four agencies providing community education, case management, and interpretation in forty-one languages, benefiting nearly 50,000 persons each year), immigrant health care at five suburban clinics newly impacted by the foreign-born, and a Refugee and Immigrant Citizenship Initiative. RICI involves English language and civics instruction, and preparation for the naturalization examinations. It incorporates pro bono legal oversight by the National Immigrant Justice Center. RICI also enabled a range of studies that have advanced the understanding of immigrant needs and characteristics. A study of taxes paid by immigrants demonstrated that the foreign-born—10 percent of the population at the time—paid 10.6 percent of Illinois taxes, and that immigrants paid twice as much in taxes for each $1 of public services as did native-born. A demographic study by a state legislative district illustrated the dispersion of the foreign-born and revealed more than 640,000 naturalized voters spread throughout the metropolitan area. The result, once immigration was considered a Chicago issue, thus a Democratic party issue, and now it is perceived as a bipartisan issue. Republican leadership was instrumental in setting state funded immigrant services in place.

In 2000, the Bureau formed four interagency work groups: Education, Health and Human Services, Employment and Economic Development, and Immigration Law. Four reports citing the needs of immigrants, the barriers they confront, and recommendations for policymakers were issued in 2003. These reports gave rise to further dialogue. The Chicago Council on Global Affairs convened year-long work groups that issued reports on immigration reform, as well as the needs of the Mexican and Muslim communities. The Illinois Department of Human Services convened a work group looking at policy and procedure across six divisions, aimed at improving access and quality of care for limited-English proficient customers.

Based on the work at IDHS, Governor Blagojevich, the son of immigrants, issued an executive order establishing the Office of New Americans Policy and Advocacy with four objectives: to create an interagency task force of state agencies to examine, department by department, how state government can systematically address the changing demographics of Illinois; to convene a council of community leaders and national experts to recommend changes in program and policy; to monitor federal law and policy changes and advise the governor; and to participate in the national discourse on immigrant integration.

In 2006, for Phase One, ten state human service agencies met to formulate policy recommendations. In 2007, for Phase Two, another nine agencies met. The interagency workgroups were organized to ensure that state services will be provided to all residents in an innovative, effective, and efficient way, including adequate language services for the limited-English proficient residents. Recommendations speak to the need for access to trained interpreters, the deployment of bilingual staff, the development of translated program materials, expanded outreach and community education, as well as an increase in English language training resources. In 2007, the first Illinois Welcome Center was established in suburban Melrose Park to provide one-stop, bilingual service coordination. Following the lead of Illinois, Massachusetts and New Jersey have embarked on a similar initiative. Maryland and New York also have developed an immigrant service initiative, but of less scope.

The New Americans Interagency Task Force Report, Phase Two, involved the Illinois State Police, a multifaceted agency, enforcing the laws, protecting the public, and providing assistance and an array of specialty services to other law enforcement agencies. The Report identifies ISP Best Practices, including community partnerships, liaison to the Hispanic community addressing crime prevention and intervention, safety education officers providing community and media liaison in twenty-one areas, online bilingual outreach material, bilingual trooper bonus compensation, access to a twenty-four hour interpretation and translation Language Line, and the equipping of each mobile unit with simultaneous translation and communication capabilities. ISP future efforts include expanding the translation services to languages other than Spanish, the increased recruitment of bilingual officers, continuation of Conversational Spanish for ISP cadets, development of cultural competency training curricula for local and state police officers, development of language booklets and technology to assist officers in communicating with the limited-English proficient population, and establishing three demonstration projects to build strong police-immigrant relations.

Education and Healthcare

The two largest arenas affecting state and local governments because of immigration are education and health care. In addition to the growing need to recruit foreign educated high skilled labor, it is quite clear that retaining foreign-born students educated in American universities should be a priority. The National Science Foundation found foreign nationals in graduate programs as follows:

	Computer Science	Electrical Engineering
Indiana University	63% (foreign)	71%
University of Texas	67%	76%
Rice University	67%	56%
Univ. of Southern Cal.	80%	78%
Univ. of Arizona	57%	86%

This brief selection indicates the high foreign-born participation rate; it might also be a statement about the education system's preparation of American students for those professions. That foreign students are paying their own way makes them attractive to the universities.

One out of every five children in the United States is the child of immigrants. For those who are English language learners, there is a great need for pre-kindergarten instruction, so that the children can be productive students when they enter formal education. For those students in K-12, there is need for enhanced English language training and tutorial support. A number of schools around the nation, including Illinois, have established Newcomer Centers to deal with the educational, cultural, and social needs of the newest arrivals. These children are a part of our future workforce.

As a side note, let us go back to 1990. There were 2 million undocumented immigrants. Many were refugees from Central America who fled their homelands in the early 1980s. In the Immigration Reform and Control Act of 1986, eligibility for adjustment of status had a cutoff entry date before January 1, 1982, thus the Central Americans entering between that date and the autumn of 1986 were ineligible for legalization. Moreover, a large portion of the 2 million was itinerant farm workers. For decades, they worked their way north from Texas ending in Michigan, and they returned home after the final harvest. Congress's response to the 2 million was to invest $40 billion in border patrol. It then became too dangerous or costly (in payment to the "coyotes" or smugglers) to return to Mexico, in particular. If they were going to stay, they wanted their families to be with them. In the end, $40 billion was spent and growth of the undocumented reached 12 million in the year 2000.

Uncounted numbers of undocumented K-12 students were brought at a very young age. They have grown up American without indigenous ties to their parents' homeland. Many have grown up undocumented living side by side with American-born citizen siblings. In order to pursue higher education, the undocumented in most states must pay out-of-state tuitions that put the pursuit beyond their means. Undocumented immigrants who have completed high school in Illinois, however, are eligible for in-state college tuition.

In Chicago, there is an ordinance that prohibits certifying immigration status in the provision of city services. First issued as an executive order by Mayor Washington and reissued by Mayor Daley, the ordinance was recently enacted by the city council to strengthen its implementation. On one hand, it is an effort to prevent racial profiling and discrimination. On the other hand, it is an effort to establish trust in city workers. Because of this policy, it is likely that undocumented immigrants access state- and city-funded English language training, which offers the opportunity for professional growth.

A favorite myth of the immigration restrictionists is that undocumented immigrants abuse and overuse public services, including health care. The fact is that the welfare and immigration reforms of 1996 barred most immigrants, including those who entered legally, from federally funded benefits. The state of Illinois uses the federal SAVE system (Systematic Alien Verification of Eligibility) in processing non-citizen applications for federal cash and medical benefits. The results are not reported to Homeland Security. However, undocumented parents are able to enroll citizen children on cash assistance without fear of status disclosure. In Illinois, all children are eligible for the All Kids medical assistance program without regard to immigration status.

The welfare reform act of 1996—the Personal Responsibility and Work Opportunity Reconciliation Act, Pub. L.No. 104-193,—created deep problems with access to medical assistance by severely limiting non-citizenship eligibility for federal benefits for at least five years. For example, if an immigrant enters with a visa to work, is here less than five years, loses employment, has medical needs, he or she is not eligible for Medicaid. All immigrants, including visitors, are eligible for Emergency Medicaid. However, if the patient is then in need of rehabilitation services, he or she is not eligible for assistance. Similarly, undocumented individuals with mental health issues can receive emergency care but have no access to community care for the long-term rehabilitation process. The ostensible effort to save money resulted in a mean-spirited disenfranchisement of foreign-born individuals with critical needs.

In addition to the issue of medical costs, a long-term effort in Illinois has focused on medical interpretation. In 1990, the Bureau participated in an interagency workgroup staffed by the Midwest Institute for Urban Poverty devoted to Immigrant and Refugee Healthcare. Hospitals were surveyed to assess their interpreter policies and resources, and promote awareness of the need. In 1992, the state legislature enacted a Language Access law. The workgroup developed a handbook for health care providers and HMOs to promote cultural and linguistic competency. Substantial progress has been made by health care providers in the past decade to address the interpretation and translation needs of limited English proficient patients.

More recently, another interagency group has worked with the Division of Mental Health and the Division of Alcohol and Substance Abuse to educate service providers and encourage planning to accommodate the needs of limited-English proficient customers. The Bureau provided startup funding for what is now Cross Cultural Interpreter Services, a nonprofit program that provides interpreter training for those working in the health, mental health, and legal arenas, as well as providing interpreter and translation services. Currently, the Metropolitan Chicago Healthcare Council is working to secure cost-effective interpreter services through video networking.

Another case in point of public policy that flies in the face of reason is the failure to provide drivers' licenses or certificates to the undocumented. Common sense and a basic interest in public safety dictate that we do not want untrained drivers on the road, and we do not want uninsured drivers on the road. It could not be clearer. Instead of a public safety issue, the provision of licenses or certification to the undocumented has become a political issue. It will take strong leadership and intensive public education to take the issue out of the political arena at the state level, just as it will at the national level, to enact meaningful, practical, and humane immigration reform.

Benefits of Facilitating Immigration

Due to low birth rates and an aging population, immigration is critical to the workforce and economies of the industrialized nations. Further, in Illinois we have experienced out-migration of the native born. In the past twenty years, approximately 2 million residents have left the state for the Sunbelt and elsewhere. They have been replaced by almost an equal number of immigrants. In the past ten years, two of every three new jobs has been filled by an immigrant. In addition, it is clear that immigrants are highly entrepreneurial. According to data from the Migration Policy Institute, in 2002 the 1.6 million Hispanic-owned businesses and 1.1 million Asian-owned businesses together had gross receipts of $548 billion and payroll of $92.7 billion.

The immigrants, including the undocumented, are here and essential. The question then is: Do we provide welcome and facilitate "integration"? As nicely define by Grantmakers Concerned with Immigrants and Refugees, "Immigrant and refugee integration is a two-way process in which newcomers and the receiving society work together to build secure, vibrant, and cohesive communities. As an intentional effort, integration engages and transforms all community members, reaping shared benefits and creating a new whole that is greater than the sum of its parts. Mutual responsibility, multi-sector involvement, public-private partnership, and a multi-strategy approach should be the cornerstones."

State and local government cannot meet the challenge of integrating the newcomers alone. It must be a public-private partnership. It must provide for intergroup dialogue, such as found in the Chicago Coalition of African, Arab, Asian, European, and Latino Immigrants of Illinois, or the Illinois Coalition for Immigrant and Refugee Rights (ICIRR). ICIRR has grown from a core of eighteen agencies to an umbrella for more than 130 agencies devoted to serving ethnic communities. It has been a major advocate for effective immigration policies and maintains a strong voice in city and state policy making. The challenge also must include the legal community in preserving civil and human rights, as well as in providing guidance to the community-based organizations that are essential to educating and serving the immigrants. The Illinois Department of Human Services has a long-term investment in the capacity building of those organizations, many of which were major English-language training sites to facilitate the 1986 legalization process. The CBOs are critical to the provision of cost-effective, culturally and linguistically appropriate services that enable immigrant economic self-sufficiency, social self-reliance, and civic participation. Those partnerships have been central to Illinois' leadership in promoting immigrant integration and vibrant, multiethnic communities.

In the words of the *New York Times* columnist Frank Rich, there is a pervasive "fear of illegal immigrants who do the low-paying jobs that Americans don't want to do and of legal immigrants who do the high-paying jobs that poorly educated Americans are not qualified to do." It is past time for us as a nation to deal with that fear in a constructive, practical manner, to enact humane and fair-minded immigration reform, and to promote immigrant integration and civic participation. In the past, immigrants have built this nation. Immigrants and their children remain essential to our future.

Edwin B. Silverman received his bachelor's degree from Purdue University and his doctorate from Northwestern University. He has been employed by the state of Illinois since 1973. From 1976 until 1997, he administered the Illinois Refugee Resettlement

Program, which became part of the Illinois Department of Public Aid in 1980. In 1997, the program became part of the Illinois Department of Human Services, and he continues to administer it as the chief of the Bureau of Refugee & Immigrant Services. He has actively participated in the development of program and policy at the federal level, and contributed to the drafting of the Refugee Act. He is president emeritus and active on the executive board for SCORR, the national affiliation of State Coordinators of Refugee Resettlement. He has received awards from the federal government, the United Nations High Commissioner for Refugees (UNHCR), and various community groups for his contributions to the area of refugee resettlement. He also received the Assistant Secretary's Public Service Award from DHHS and was one of five national recipients in 1995 of the American Society for Public Administration's National Public Service Award.

Seeking a Way to Enact Reform That Helps, Rather Than Hinders, Immigrants

Norman Levine

State Refugee Coordinator

New Mexico Human Services Department

ASPATORE

I pity the poor immigrant
Who tramples through the mud,
Who fills his mouth with laughing
And who builds his town with blood,
Whose visions in the final end
Must shatter like the glass.
I pity the poor immigrant
When his gladness comes to pass

Bob Dylan

No issue in contemporary America is surrounded by more intense emotion, is the subject of more misconceptions, and seems less likely to be resolved, than that of what should be our national immigration policy.

The current tide of immigrants, both legal and illegal, increasingly diversifies the American ethnic, racial, and religious profile in an economic environment that continuously places less value on the jobs that were once the point of entry into self-sufficiency for immigrants. This tide also increases the competition for those jobs that exists between citizens and immigrants, and the government at all levels is being challenged to respond.

Current immigration law, unlike that of many nations such as Canada, does not, for the most part, utilize selection criteria such as age, employability, language competency, and educational achievement in identifying those who will be admitted from the total pool of those seeking to immigrate to the United States. Additionally, unlike many western nations, the United States does not provide an initial structured acculturation period to newly arrived immigrants, or provide transitional financial assistance to those in need. As a result, immigrants enter into a "sink or swim" environment when they reach these shores, and must rely for survival on themselves, their families, their ethnic and religious communities, and the private social service sector, with minimal governmental assistance.

Since the passage of the *Personal Responsibility and Work Act of 1996 (Public Law 104-193)* most legal immigrants have been specifically barred from receiving benefits from almost all federally funded entitlement programs for at least their first five years in the United States. All illegal immigrants are permanently barred from these programs. With these bars in place, employment, and hopefully access to employer-provided health care insurance, is the immigrants' sole source to provide food, clothing, shelter, and health care for their families and themselves. Without access to employment or the "safety net" programs, government at all levels must find ways of improving timely access to employment leading to economic self-sufficiency, or be faced with a permanent immigrant underclass.

Complicating the situation are the changing patterns of immigration to the United States, with increasing percentages arriving from non-European nations. As more people of color or believers in non-Judeo Christian religions reach these shores, a revival of nativist ideology is an appropriate response from many to the demographic changes they see around them. For others, in a heightened atmosphere of fear of strangers, restricting access to our shores seems appropriate.

Additionally, as immigration policy becomes a "hot-button" issue, the various paths to immigration to the United States get lost in the shouting. The distinctions between legal and illegal immigrants tend to disappear, and all immigrants tend to face an uncomfortable and distrustful environment.

For any government to act responsibly in the face of these challenges, some degree of national consensus on appropriate goals and reasonable means to achieve them is essential. However, in an environment in which ant-immigrant sentiment is rife, achieving such a consensus is difficult, and Congress and the president quickly backpedaled from trying to develop a bipartisan comprehensive approach to immigration reform. They have adopted a piecemeal approach that is weighted heavily toward border security issues, and ignores all other aspects of this complex problem.

Recently, in the absence of comprehensive federal action, states, city, county, and town governments have responded to what they perceive to be an unchecked wave of undocumented immigrants by passing laws to control their access to employment and housing.

At the federal, state, and local levels, these narrow and targeted attempts to respond to what everyone concedes is a broken immigration system, have only led to increased confusion between legal and illegal immigrants, and the establishment of what may become significant barriers to legal immigrants receiving fair and equitable treatment under the law.

At the time of their entry into the United States, legal immigrants receive the specific entry documents called for in the Immigration and Naturalization Act (INA) (*8 USC*) that define their legal status and confirm their identity. Most people not in everyday contact with immigrants assume that the I-551 Permanent Resident Card, better known as the "green card," is the universal identifier of legal immigrants. As a result, many of these recent laws that require immigrants to show "official identification" to take part in many activities of daily life, have created major barriers to their achieving early integration into our communities by making many of the documents provided to lawful immigrants insufficient to achieve the purposes for which they were intended.

Examples of the unintended consequences for immigrants of recent governmental initiatives to control immigration are:

The Immigration Reform and Control Act Of 1986 (IRCA) (8 USC 1001)

More than twenty years ago, Congress passed IRCA, which for the first time placed the onus for identifying lawful employees on employers by establishing the concept of "employer sanctions." Employer sanctions were based on the theory that employers would only hire work-eligible individuals if they faced financial penalties for hiring undocumented workers, and by reducing job opportunities for the undocumented, the U.S. would become a much less attractive place for migrants.

In concept, employer sanctions could reach the desired goal of reducing illegal immigration. However, without strict and consistent enforcement, employer sanctions could also lead to workplace discrimination against, and ultimately exploitation of, both legal and illegal immigrants. *See Hoffman Plastic Compounds Inc v NLRB*, 535 U.S. 137 (2002).

To its credit, Congress recognized that hiring discrimination against foreign-born persons legally authorized to work could result from the passage of IRCA, and therefore included in the law a mandate that the

General Accounting Office (GAO) conduct a longitudinal study of the impact of Employer Sanctions.

The GAO report, released in March 1990, described a widespread pattern of hiring discrimination against both legal and illegal immigrants. Almost 20 percent of the 4.5 million employers surveyed by the GAO indicated that in response to IRCA, they had initiated such practices as hiring only those who could prove they were born in the United States, not hiring persons with accents, or rejecting some valid immigration documents as proof of work eligibility. Given that this finding was based on employers' self-reporting, it is very possible that the actual rate of bias against immigrants in the hiring process is significantly higher.

The validity of the GAO findings is supported by other contemporaneous studies (e.g., *Tarnishing the Golden Door, New York City Commission on Human Rights*, 1989) which found very similar rates of employer discrimination against immigrants. Rather than initiate action to combat discrimination and protect immigrant rights, Congress amended the law in 1990 to include criminal penalties for "document fraud." As a result, employers were now in a position to defend themselves against Employer Sanctions by claiming the persons they hired used fraudulent documents to prove employment eligibility, thereby shifting almost all responsibility away from employers and onto immigrants.

Apparently, enforcement of the employer sanctions provisions was never given a high priority by immigration officials. In 2003, of the almost 22,000 investigations conducted by Immigration and Customs Enforcement (ICE), only 124 resulted in employer sanctions being levied.

However, ICE has increasingly initiated large-scale raids of job sites, particularly in the meatpacking industry. These have resulted in hundreds of aliens being detained and charged with document fraud, but only rarely a case in which employer sanctions have been imposed.

The consequences of these trends for lawful immigrants seeking employment are severe. Many "good" employers find it convenient to avoid hiring immigrants, while the unscrupulous feel little risk in hiring and exploiting both legal and illegal immigrants.

E-Verify

Employment authorization verification was required by IRCA, and the I-9 verification process in which all prospective employees, native or foreign-born, are required to complete a standard form and present a series of documents from among a specified list. Employers are required to maintain files containing the I-9s and associated documentation. Seeking to improve on the I-9 process, several years ago the Department of Homeland Security (DHS) initiated the voluntary, Web-based Basic Pilot system, through which potential employers could, as an alternative to using I-9s, verify the immigration status and employment eligibility of candidates for employment as required by IRCA. Although there is much evidence that the database used in the Basic Pilot is neither complete nor accurate, DHS has chosen to roll out E-Verify, a slightly updated version of the Basic Pilot.

Currently, approximately 70,000 employers have enrolled in E-Verify. As many as 200,000 employers with federal contracts will be required to do so by a June 9, 2008, Executive Order.

While using E-Verify is still voluntary at the federal level, except for federal contractors, several states have already begun mandating that employers within their borders utilize it, with the threat of revoking business licenses as the penalty for non-compliance. While some employers will comply, others will try to find ways to avoid the administrative costs of such a system, and find subtle ways, even in the face of anti-employment discrimination laws, to not accept persons as viable job candidates who identify themselves as immigrants, speak with a foreign accent, or present non-U.S. work experience.

E-Verify is based on information provided and immigration documents presented by the potential employee to the employer in the mandatory I-9 Employment Eligibility Verification process. However, potential errors leading to a non-verification outcome are myriad. A simple transposition of a number or the misspelling of a name (either by the potential employer inputting the data into E-Verify, or by DHS and the Social Security Administration (SSA) in creating the database entry) will cause a mismatch with the DHS database.

When such mismatches occur, much of the burden of correcting mistakes, particularly those resulting from data entry problems by DHS or SSA, falls primarily on the immigrant applicant. The immigrant, often with few English language skills, must contact the federal agency and attempt to get the database error corrected. While this process is going on, the employer may look to another candidate who presents no employment eligibility verification problems.

Additionally, as legal immigrants enter the United States at multiple points of entry and in a variety of immigration statuses (often with unique forms of documentation of status), compiling and maintaining a database that is both timely and accurate is a daunting task. Even though legal immigrants are authorized to work from the moment of admission by the INA, a paperwork transmittal or database entry delay could prevent an immigrant from being employed, due to the inability of E-Verify to provide an affirmative verification for some period of time after a lawful admission to the United States.

Compounding this situation is the fact that the SSA will not issue a Social Security card until it has verified the lawful immigration status of each applicant, a process that often results in delaying receipt of the Social Security card for up to six weeks.

With all its flaws and potential negative consequences for immigrants, E-Verify seems on course to be the primary tool in determining who can work and who cannot. However, the federal government does not seem to be totally reliant on E-Verify for all status verification processes, and has established a second database for immigrants, the Systematic Alien Verification for Entitlements (SAVE). States are required to use the SAVE system when a non-citizen applies for any state-administered, federally funded benefit. The SAVE system, unlike E-Verify, allows for a secondary verification system and even a non-electronic manual process that can be initiated when there is not an initial eligibility determination.

The Real ID Act of 1985

The Real ID Act (Division D of the Emergency Supplemental Appropriations Act for Defense, the Global War on Terrorism, and

Tsunami Relief, Pub. L. No. 109-13, 119 Stat. 234 (2005)) was designed to ensure that each state act to prevent terrorism, reduce fraud, and improve the reliability and accuracy of identification documents it issued, with a specific focus on driver's licenses. These have become the primary identification document required for such activities as entering federal buildings or boarding commercial aircraft. In fact, the driver's license has become the equivalent of a national identity card.

The act mandates that all applicants provide a series of source documents at the time of application that are then used for verifying identity, lawful status, date of birth, and Social Security number with the issuing agency. In response, each state has created its own list of acceptable source documents, often creating almost insurmountable barriers for whole categories of legal immigrants in securing a driver's license, which in many locales is almost a prerequisite for securing and maintaining employment. In most states, the current list of required identity documents for non-citizens typically include DHS-issued green cards and/or employment authorization documents, as well as Social Security cards and foreign birth certificates accompanied by a certified English translation.

For many lawful immigrants, particularly refugees, Cuban/Haitian entrants and asylees, their lawful entry into the United States is documented in many ways, such as I-94 Entry/Departure cards, with a stamp indicating their admission for permanent residence under a specific section of the INA, or a form or letter from DHS or an immigration judge, granting asylum. As these categories of lawful immigrants are not eligible to apply for a green card until one year after the date of admission, and are often faced with lengthy delays in receiving their Social Security cards and EADs, some or all of the required documents are not available to prove lawful status. Therefore, eligibility for a driver's license in the first weeks or months after arrival is particularly difficult, resulting in an inability to lawfully drive during a critical period for securing employment.

Additionally, as proof of identity for an immigrant requires providing a birth certificate or a valid passport from their country of origin, refugees, Cuban/Haitian entrants and asylees, are particularly disadvantaged by this process. Their lawful entry into the United States was predicated on their flight from their home country, because of actual or threatened persecution due to their race, religion, ethnicity, or political association, making the possession of a valid passport or original birth certificate virtually impossible.

Not having a valid driver's license (or state issued ID card) has additional negative consequences for immigrants, particularly those who do not have any other form of commonly recognized identification. Typically, banks are resistant to open accounts for people without state issued identification, making check cashing or securing credit almost impossible. Landlords often request a photocopy of a driver's license as part of the rental application, and a driver's license number is requested on many job application forms.

It is important to note that another federal agency, the Office of Refugee Resettlement (ORR), a part of the Administration for Children and Families (ACF) within the Department of Health and Human Services (DHHS), has promulgated rules governing acceptable identification documents for refugees, Cuban/Haitian entrants and asylees, to facilitate the processing of their applications for federally funded programs and benefits within their state of residence. These regulations have been amplified through a series of "State Letters," which provide comprehensive listings of all documentation provided to these immigrants and their relationship to program and benefit eligibility. (e.g., ORR State Letter #00-17: Status and Documentation Requirements for the Federal Refugee Resettlement Program and ORR State Letter 08-04: Consolidated Appropriations Act of 2008: Time Limited Benefits and Services For Iraqis and Afghans Granted Special Immigrant Status Under Section 101 (a)27 of the Immigration and Nationality Act)

Because of these clarifications, access to federally funded cash assistance, health care, employment, and social services is relatively barrier free for ORR's clients. In the absence of action by DHS to emulate ORR's concern for informing the states of acceptable forms of documentation, the burden of trying to get state motor vehicle departments to broaden their documentation requirements to include all federally issued lawful entry documents has fallen on local advocates and state officials assigned to administer programs for refugees, Cuban/Haitian entrants and asylees.

State and Municipal Laws

Immigration policy is clearly a function of the federal government, but immigrants live in local areas. For many reasons, their distribution across the fifty states is uneven, with some states, cities, and towns feeling a disproportionate impact as immigrants seek employment, enroll their children in schools, and introduce new cultures to their new hometowns. While local communities may have no control over who enters the country and decides to move to their jurisdiction, they are increasingly seeking to find ways to manage the impact of immigrants on their economies, social networks, and civic institutions.

Recently, state and local governments have enacted a variety of laws seeking to make it difficult for illegal immigrants to live in their jurisdictions, with the hope that they will respond by returning to their homelands. The trend toward enacting such laws seems well established, with 156 state and local laws being put on the books in 2007. States passing such laws include Arizona (Legal Arizona Workers Act AZHB2779), Colorado, Georgia, Mississippi, and Oklahoma, while local governments in such diverse locales as Valley Park, Missouri, Farmers Branch, Texas, Riverside, New Jersey, and Hazelton, Pennsylvania have enacted local immigration related ordinances.

Typically, these laws have primarily focused on limiting access to employment and housing by establishing penalties, such as loss of business licenses or being debarred from government contracts, for business owners who hire non-documented immigrants, and property owners who rent to them. One local law, Hazelton, Pennsylvania, *Hazleton v. Lozano*, No. 06-1586, 2007 U.S. Dist. LEXIS 54320 (M.D. Pa. July 26, 2007), even allows employees who have been discharged to initiate a job discrimination suit for treble damages if they claim the employer who discharged them has employed illegal immigrants at any time. Additionally, some municipalities have used zoning or other local regulations to severely limit the existence of formal or informal day laborer hiring sites.

While most, if not all, of these laws have been challenged in the courts on the grounds that immigration control is a federal function, just the fact that such laws are discussed creates an inhospitable environment for all immigrants. Anecdotal evidence from the Hazelton, Pennsylvania experience indicates that both legal and illegal immigrants left the area soon after the ordinance was passed, on the assumption that the local citizenry could not really tell the difference between the categories, and all would face increased barriers to living a normal life in the community.

Further, as the employment of immigrants is already regulated by the federal government, with stringent procedures in place for employment authorization, however flawed, additional state requirements seem redundant. However, as federal enforcement of its own laws and regulations has been inconsistent at best, and confidence in the government's ability to maintain control over immigration is low, these state and municipal laws seem to be an attempt to convey to the public a message that "someone is doing something" about the problem.

It is ironic that state and local officials, with little trust in the federal system, then enact laws that must of necessity rely on the E-Verify system with all of its shortcomings, including time lags and data entry problems, as the primary component of their new employment verification system. As was the case with the initial federal employment verification requirements, employers presented with new administrative mandates from the state may choose to limit their hiring to people who do not give the appearance of being immigrants, or simply cut back on their productive capacity. This last option has been taken by a number of farmers in the face of what they see to be a system that makes it difficult for them to easily engage enough labor to tend their fields or harvest their crops.

As to laws governing rental of apartments to illegal immigrants, even though the constitutionality of these laws is often successfully challenged in the courts, they tend to have a negative impact on all immigrants seeking housing. Property owners who are not experts in deciphering immigration documents are being asked to verify, without access to even a flawed database such as E-Verify, the lawful status of rental applicants or face significant penalties. In communities impacted by immigrants, not renting to non-English speakers or people of color may seem to be an attractive alternative to establishing a document verification system, particularly when most, if not all immigrants, do not have the knowledge or ability to begin a housing discrimination procedure.

Where local governments have tried to limit the employment of day laborers, perhaps under the assumption that all day laborers are illegally in the United States, and in the face of a long constitutional understanding that the act of soliciting work is protected free speech, the courts have typically not upheld the laws. However, by creating a climate of distrust and fear, these communities may very well succeed in reducing their immigrant populations, including a significant portion of their lawful immigrant residents.

Recommended Strategies

As more and more people openly question the legal presence among us of non-English speakers (particularly Hispanics) and people of color; as the current economic downturn puts large segments of our population at significant risk of losing their jobs, their homes, and their futures; and as the basic fabric of our society changes to include a diverse array of new cultural practices, it has become more acceptable to blame the strangers among us for our problems.

With all the emphasis that has been placed on border control and reducing the number of undocumented workers, seemingly little thought has been given to the plight of many of the legal immigrants we welcome to our shores each year, who need gainful employment to survive. At a point in time when whole industries, particularly agribusiness, are facing massive labor shortages that threaten their capacity to produce, it would seem appropriate to implement a series of strategic initiatives to facilitate immigrant access to a job market that needs them.

1. The Department of Homeland Security needs to create a single, tamper-proof document, containing biometric information, which all lawful immigrants receive at the time of entry. While the various immigration statuses may differ and be coded accordingly, a single document would greatly simplify immigrants' access to employment, driver's licenses, banking, and other vital services, as employers and service providers would then not be faced with the current array of admission documents when determining an alien's eligibility.

2. The Department of Homeland Security and the Social Security need to find ways to reduce the time it takes to generate essential documents for immigrants. As almost all immigrants, except Cuban/Haitian entrants and asylees, arrive in the United States with significant advance notice, there is no reason that documents could not be available to them either at the time of admission or within a few days of admission. For Cuban/Haitian entrants and asylees, document processing must become a priority, as early employment is essential to their futures.

3. Every effort must be made to ensure that every entry into the E-Verify database is accurate and timely, to minimize the possibilities of incorrect mismatches. With current technology, it should be possible to immediately incorporate into the database electronic copies of all documents presented to immigrants, so that data input errors are minimized.

4. Improve communications between federal and state labor departments and employers, regarding their rights and responsibilities in employing immigrants

5. As part of the immigration process, the federal government and all its involved departments need to expand pre-arrival cultural orientation programs, to better prepare immigrants for the tasks they will face on entry into the U.S. A series of post-arrival follow-ups could be of great help in assisting immigrants in identifying resources they might need to resolve problems they are facing in their acculturation process.

6. Expand the linkages between the federal immigration authorities and the not-for-profit and religious sectors, to provide additional assistance to immigrants. This type of public-private partnership is already used to great benefit in the refugee resettlement program, which could provide a replicable model for additional acculturation services to immigrants.

7. At the state and local level, expand existing English as a Second Language programs to facilitate the learning of English.

8. Federal, state, and local authorities need to develop public education programs that focus on educating the community as to exactly who immigrants are, what their rights are, and what they contribute to the general well-being of our nation and communities.

9. State officials and immigrants' rights advocates must work to ensure immigrants receive all the benefits and services they are entitled to under existing laws, and seek to remove barriers that prevent immigrants from fully participating in our society.

Looking Ahead

There is little question that most immigrants are facing new, and some times almost insurmountable, barriers to successfully entering into mainstream America. As the threat of terrorism, a weakening economy, and a slow but steady evolution of traditional ways of life threaten the security of many Americans, immigrants become an increasingly acceptable target for blame.

After the events of September 11, 2001 the palpable fear of another terrorist attack on our homeland has put immigrants under a cloud of suspicion and put them in the middle of a no-win debate over how many of our constitutional rights can be abridged to ensure our safety. Until we, as a nation, find ways to successfully combat global terrorism without surrendering our essential freedoms, it is unclear that any national initiatives to make America more "immigrant friendly" can gain wide public acceptance. Therefore, in the short term at least, securing a bipartisan congressional agreement on comprehensive immigration reform legislation will be almost impossible to achieve.

And, if the recent trend toward immigration legislation that only focuses on controlling our borders continues and removing undocumented workers from our fields and factories, legal immigrants will likely continue to get caught up in the backwash as without a concomitant commitment of resources to provide them with the documentation that they need and protect their rights to employment and housing, many may fall through the cracks in the system.

Within the context of federal inaction, it will then be up to our states and cities to respond to the needs of their immigrant residents. For example, states such as New York and Illinois, and cities like San Francisco have made significant commitments to finding ways to ensure that immigrants maintain access to services and are protected from discrimination.

New York State, through its Bureau of Refugee and Immigrant Affairs (BRIA), provides a clearinghouse to help immigrants identify and access available services and produces native language materials to support this effort. Additionally BRIA helps local community based agencies respond to their immigrant populations and assists in helping immigrants transition to their new lives. A telephone hotline with the capability to respond in seventeen languages assists immigrants with citizenship and immigration issues as well as providing help in completing applications.

The "New Americans Executive Order," announced by Illinois Governor Rod Blagojevich in late 2005, established the Office of New Americans Policy and Advocacy to coordinate all aspects of state government policy and planning related to immigrant integration within the state and created a public-private state task force to examine department by department how state government can better address the needs of Illinois' immigrant population. Additionally, the state spends more than $3 million each year, through a grant to the Illinois Coalition for Immigrant and Refugee Rights, to assist eligible permanent residents become naturalized U.S. citizens.

The city of San Francisco has enacted a local ordinances designed to protect immigrant rights, ensure that city services are appropriately delivered, and open immigrants' access to services. Replication of this type of local initiatives would provide immigrants with an invaluable tool to help ensure that their rights are not abridged and that access to services to which they are entitled by law is barrier free.

State and local leaders should follow the example of Michael Bloomberg, mayor of the city of New York, and call public attention to the significant contributions immigrants make to the economy and vitality of their communities. With this type of leadership, perhaps some of the negative attitudes toward immigrants can be ameliorated and additional local initiatives enacted to facilitate immigrant acculturation.

However, despite the good intentions of many communities and politicians, the direction of our economy in the coming years may play the leading role in deciding the direction of the immigration debate.

There is little question that immigrants fill low paying jobs, often because non-immigrants in the work force choose to seek employment in other less physically demanding and often more lucrative fields. A 2005 study by the Pew Hispanic Center utilizing census data determined that 7.2 million undocumented persons were in the labor force, representing just under 5 percent of all workers. Pew Hispanic Center Research Report, *The Size and Characteristics of Unauthorized Migrant Population in the United States*, March 2006.Of particular interest was the concentration of the undocumented in just a few employment sectors: 24 percent of all farm workers, 17 percent of all cleaning workers, 14 percent of all construction workers, and 12 percent of all food preparation workers.

As unemployment rises bringing with it higher levels of economic insecurity, immigrants will almost certainly absorb a disproportionate impact. Already we have evidence that the immigrant community is feeling the impact of the economic slowdown. Remittances to Mexico and Central American countries have shown a significant decrease as both legal and undocumented workers lose their jobs and there is anecdotal evidence that some immigrants are beginning to return home.

It is possible that the combination of a poor economy and increased law enforcement at the border and job sites may serve as the most effective immigration control mechanism we have.

Yet while many key industries—manufacturing and residential construction, for example—are shedding jobs at a significant rate, others like the high tech sector and agriculture are facing labor shortages and repeatedly make a claim for an increased supply of imported labor through an expansion of the HI and H2 visa programs.

Within this context, good public policy would seem to call for a more rational immigration system that would be responsive to fluctuations in the economy and the job market. Given the nature of immigrant employment, an immigration system that would allow those undocumented immigrants who are already in the workforce to have a path toward qualifying for legal status would make sense.

If such policies were coupled with a realistic living minimum wage standard, access to universal health insurance, and increased opportunities to access for job training programs which enhance the capabilities of the present domestic labor force we would be better able to redeploy the existing labor supply to areas of need and increase productivity.

However, rather than develop such policies, some have proposed the establishment of short-term, employer friendly "guest worker" programs to meet critical labor shortages. Historically, when such programs are instituted, minimally skilled workers, including immigrants, are forced to compete with "guest workers" for jobs that have low wages and no benefits. One only has to look at the history of the "Bracero Program," which between 1942 and 1964 allowed some 4.5 million Mexican farm workers into the United States as temporary agricultural laborers, to see their impact.

Although the agreement between the governments of the United States and Mexico stipulated that "braceros" were not to be brought into areas where domestic labor was available and were be paid the prevailing wage for agricultural work in the region, but not less than fifty cents per hour, the minimum wage of fifty cents per hour became the maximum wage offered. If domestic laborers refused to accept such low wages, local officials would claim a shortage of laborers and request even more braceros. As a result, many domestic laborers who might have worked in agriculture for a decent wage were displaced by Mexican nationals. With little governmental monitoring of the program there is no question that many "braceros" were cheated and abused. In fact, the U.S. Department of Labor officer in charge of the program, Lee G. Williams, was quoted as describing the "Bracero Program" as a form of "legalized slavery."

It is likely that should "guest worker" programs be reestablished, many of the faults of the previous programs will be repeated as there seems to be little governmental concern for regulating businesses and recognizing or enforcing workers' rights.

Perhaps the simplest and most easily accomplished step that could benefit immigrants is the simplification of the documentation they are provided to identify their immigration status and authorization to work. Such a change would not require passage of new laws but would need regulatory revisions. However, as currently fees are attached to each immigration application and transaction, and these funds are used to help sustain the U.S. Citizenship and Immigration Service (USCIS), there is little likelihood that simplification resulting in a reduction of fee income, will take place.

Both the proponents and opponents of a more realistic immigration system agree that our current immigration system is broken. However, despite the heated rhetoric and political jockeying, the most we can expect is that tinkering will be done around the margins and no one will walk away happy, particularly the immigrants we have welcomed to our shores.

Related Resources

Discrimination Against Immigrant Employees

Hoffman Plastic Compounds Inc v NLRB, 535 U.S. 137 (2002)
Tarnishing the Golden Door, New York City Commission on Human Rights, 1989
San Francisco Immigrants Rights Commission Compliance Checklist, 2005

Immigrant Status Verification

Legal Arizona Workers Act AZHB2779
71 C.F.R.. 37281 (June. 14, 2006). (Proposed Rule for Safe Harbor for Employers Who Receive a No-Match Letter)

72 C.F.R. 45611 (Aug. 15, 2007) (Final Rule for Safe Harbor for Employers Who Receive a No-Match Letter)
AFL/CIO et al v Chertoff et al (N.D. Cal. Case No. 07-CV-4472 CRB). (Request for a Temporary Restraining Order to prevent implementation of *72* Fed. Reg. 45611)
8 C.F.R.. Part 274a (Revised Final Rule for Safe Harbor for Employers Who Receive a No-Match Letter in response to *AFL/CIO et al v Chertoff et al*))

State and Local Laws

Hazleton v. Lozano, No. 06-1586, 2007 U.S. Dist. LEXIS 54320 (M.D. Pa. July 26, 2007
Stewart v. Cherokee County, Ga., No. 07-0015 (N.D. Ga., complaint filed January 4, 2007)
Villas at Parkside Partners v. City of Farmers Branch, No. 06-2371, 2007 U.S. Dist. LEXIS 46508
(N.D. Tex. June 26, 2007)
Reynolds v. City of Valley Park, No. 06-3802 (Cir. Ct. St Louis, Mo.(March 12, 2007)
Garrett v. City of Escondido, No. 06-2434 (S.D. Cal. 2006)

Statistical Profile

The Size and Characteristics of Unauthorized Migrant Population in the United States, Pew Hispanic Center Research Report, March 2006

Born and raised in New York City, Norman Levine is the state refugee coordinator of the New Mexico Human Services Department. Mr. Levine received a B.A. in sociology from Hunter College of the City University of New York in 1964 and an M.S.W. from the University of Pennsylvania School of Social Work in 1966.

From 1966 to 1986, Mr. Levine worked in community-based social service agencies in the United States and Canada. In 1987, Mr. Levine joined the Hebrew Immigrant Aid Society (HIAS) as the assistant director of Field Operations for the Refugee Resettlement Program. In 1990, he became director of Field Operations where he oversaw a program that included a national network of more than one hundred resettlement affiliates *resettling more than 320,000 refugees from around the world during his tenure with annual expenditures of more than $20 million.*

After leaving HIAS in 2002, Mr. Levine served as a consultant to state governments and not-for-profit agencies including the New York State Bureau of Refugee and Immigrant Affairs, the New York State Department of Motor Vehicles, the United Jewish Federation of Northeastern New York, and the New Mexico Engineering Foundation.

In September 2006, Mr. Levine was appointed to the position of New Mexico state refugee coordinator.

Political Pressures on Immigration Reform

James R. Edwards Jr.
Principal
The MITA Group

ASPATORE

Immigration and Politics

The emerging immigration issues last year included the concerted commitment by the administration to enforce current law. Also, there was a rising number of efforts at the state and local level, ordinances, and state laws to address the fallout immigration is having at those levels. Those kinds of enforcement activities gained a secure foothold. These two issues emerged because last year the U.S. Senate attempted a major legislative push for comprehensive immigration reform. When that failed to pass the Senate in the early summer of 2007, the steam left the advocates' side, and resulted in a sense of "Well, what next?" Because little "legislative steam" remained, the administration decided to step up enforcement. What emerged last year after the big legislative fight played out was a combination of the federal side concertedly enforcing current law, and the state and local legislative activity to deal with the peripheral issues that are the consequences of immigration. For instance, Immigration and Customs Enforcement stepped up workplace enforcement. ICE staged arrests at such worksites as Swift meatpacking plants, Bianco Inc. factories, and Agriprocessors worksites. Some thirty-five state legislatures considered nearly 200 immigration enforcement bills. Several states, including Oklahoma, enacted broad measures to crack down on illegal immigrants in their borders.

The issue of whether having different laws from state to state makes immigration enforcement more difficult depends on the point of view of those involved. An employer with multiple facilities needs to comply with the rules of each specific locality in which he operates. John Q. Citizen is hardly affected. Those in law enforcement will only be able to perform the enforcement activity authorized in their jurisdiction, but that should not complicate things. Further, they possess "inherent authority" to assist in federal law enforcement (covered later). What it does is make employment and housing and health care more complicated and difficult for illegal immigrants, and tends to drive them to move to locations more lax in enforcement, or to drive them out of the country altogether.

Politically, the trend has been remarkable growth in state and local action related to immigration. People have become entirely fed up with changes in their communities, which are the consequences of mass immigration and illegality by foreigners occurring at the grassroots level. For example, there have been many instances of drunk driving by illegal aliens killing local people, as occurred in prominent cases in Charlotte, North Carolina, and the Norfolk, Virginia area, rising foreign gang presence in schools and towns, and a seemingly overnight presence of large cadres of foreign-speaking people imported to work at certain plants locally. So throughout the country, states, counties, cities, and towns have taken action to deal with the ramifications of immigration, such as overcrowded houses, farm animals kept at suburban houses, unkempt yards, and increased litter. People have demanded a crackdown through local action on unscrupulous employers that have an illegal workforce or largely so, to prohibit renting to illegals, and similar actions. Politically, that has driven much of the local and state action. The rapid rise in these laws indicates there is a real legitimate need which states and locals must address, caused by our present immigration system. Also, this shows it is politically desirable to be on the law-and-order side of the issue. It would not be attractive to politicians to do that if there was not real community support for what they are doing. A mayor in Pennsylvania, Lou Barletta of Hazelton, who led the charge in his town for those kinds of ordinances not only won the Republican primary for reelection, but also won the Democrat primary election by write-in. That is remarkable, telling anecdote.

Another trend relates to middle-class economic uncertainty. The country has enjoyed a number of years of sustained economic growth. Until the last few months of 2007 and into 2008, our country has seen sustained growth in the national economy, as measured by indicators of Dow Jones type growth and the federal reports on economic growth. Yet at the same time, there was perceived to be a lack of corresponding benefits for average Americans. We see economic prosperity for someone at the top executive and Wall Street level, but middle-class households do not feel they have benefited from it themselves. This sense rises from less than rigorous growth in wages over the last few years, working families seeing the outsourcing and off-shoring of jobs, and the importation of cheaper foreign labor, both legal and illegal, that has caused intense economic uncertainty in the middle class. This important economic trend is driving us, on the economic side, to these changes toward immigration. I think the national economic growth data belies the deep sense that people have of economic insecurity. In many instances, Americans have felt these economic shifts for a decade or more, and it has come to a head.

The social trends driving all this stem from people seeing immigrants now coming in such mass sustained numbers. It is almost unprecedented that we have such massive levels of immigration. And that means now it is hard for most average Americans not to encounter immigration's fallout themselves and see the consequences in their own lives and neighborhoods. This has even happened in suburban or rural parts of the country, and the Midwest and the South where there is not a tradition of being an immigrant landing station. People see an influx of aliens causing crowded public schools or taxing their local resources. They see a handful of immigrant children monopolizing the teacher's aide in the class, so she cannot help the other students. People see things like packed emergency rooms, and pay higher health insurance premiums or insurance becomes unaffordable, as immigration is a part of imposing uncompensated health care costs. The social trend of increasing Spanish language advertising and hearing "press one for English" sticks in people's craw. There is a real sense that something is amiss here if we are allowing immigration to overtake what it means to be an American in American society. People see in their neighborhoods overcrowded single-family homes occupied by many people unrelated to one another, with too many cars parked in front of that house, and noise and music at all hours. People see increases in crime, drugs, ID theft, Social Security theft, and fraud. All these things relate to immigration because often people who are here illegally engage in those crimes as financial supplement or to pay off the people who smuggled them in or to get a job unlawfully.

Another indicator in this social trends area has been, in the past few years, the May Day marches. Millions of illegal aliens march in American streets, demanding amnesty for their own law breaking. These demonstrations are a real affront to most Americans. Mass protest marches have helped to feed the perception that these people refuse to assimilate or Americanize. They intend to have their cake and eat it too—benefit from America's blessings without becoming Americans, and maintain strong ties to their homeland. People do not tend to buy into such behavior and aliens' attitudes as being part of the bargain from an American standpoint. It is not just native-born or long-term immigrants who have these views. Fairly recent legal immigrants are often some of the most vociferous in holding those views of rejecting foreigners' demands. "We stuck it out the right way. It was expensive and tough. Why should we be slapped in the face by allowing massive illegal immigration?" That nuance is often overlooked, but part of the churn in these emerging immigration issues.

The biggest issues we face deal with enforcement of current immigration law, because of the stepped-up enforcement actions both at the border and in the interior. In those situations, I would recommend working with law enforcement or entities supportive of the law enforcement mission. For example, one company does Web-based training for law enforcement in the immigration arena. One part of the issue is workforce related, trying to help businesses wear a white hat, those wanting to do the right thing and hire a lawful workforce, and point those law-abiding employers to the tools that can help them do that.

Employment

The pre-eminent employment-related issues are employee verification and Social Security numbers—whether the information workers have given match up with the government's records or not. On the employee verification side, this is part of the employer sanctions laws. The law struck in 1986 (Immigration Reform and Control Act, or IRCA, Public Law 99-603) had three elements. One major part was the amnesty for 3 million illegal aliens. Another part was the trade-off of employer sanctions; if you knowingly hire illegal aliens, then you would be subject to prosecution. What that became in practice was the I-9 form. When anyone, native-born or foreign-born, takes a new job, employers give him or her various forms to fill out. One is for tax withholdings and one is the I-9 form, to affirm one's eligibility to work in this country. The employer makes copies of a couple different kinds of IDs proffered. The employer attests to the I-9 and it sits in an employment file. There is little confirmation that the information is legitimate and employees are eligible to work in the country. In 1996, Congress created a pilot project to verify electronically some of the basic information on the I-9 form, such as full name, Social Security number or alien number, and so forth. 8 U.S.C. 1324a. Employers now can voluntarily participate in that program, which is becoming increasingly important. More employers are signing up, and there is increasingly legislation to eventually phase in mandatory participation by all U.S. employers.

Along with that, the Social Security Administration has in the past sent out no-match letters to inform employers that the name of an employee whose wages have been held for FICA tax do not match the Social Security number submitted. This typically might be a recently married female who has not informed the Social Security Administration of a name change, it could be an ID theft situation, or it could be an illegal alien committing Social Security fraud. Those are the emerging issues on the employment side.

Increasingly, states and localities are requiring their own agencies and those under their jurisdictions to verify employee work eligibility using the federal system of verification through electronic means, called E-Verify. This may include contractors with the state, or private contractors that do business with the local government. Local employers may be required to use E-Verify as well. On the opposite side, a few states or localities have adopted sanctuary policies—instances in the U.S. giving illegal aliens safe harbor. For example, New York City's sanctuary policy, Executive Order 124, limited police officers from inquiring into suspects' immigration status. In 1996, Congress barred such policies (§ 642 of the Illegal Immigration Reform and Immigrant Responsibility Act of 1996 (IIRIRA), Pub. L. No. 104-208). New York City sued and lost (*City of New York v. United States*, 528 U.S. 1115 (2000). Illinois attempted to enact a prohibition against verification of employees (Section 12(a) of the Illinois Right to Privacy in the Workplace Act). The U.S. Department of Homeland Security filed suit against this law, and the state was barred from enforcing the measure while it remains in litigation (*United States v. Illinois*, C.D. Ill., No. 07-3261, complaint filed 9/24/07). Such a bald-faced attempt is probably an unconstitutional act on the part of a state or locality. The California legislature is considering similar, provocative legislation. Notably, these efforts run counter to the enforcement-minded initiatives in the vast majority of states and in localities.

At the federal level, Homeland Security is now more actively promoting the E-verify program, signing up 1,000 new employers each month, so there has been a real increase in the number of participating businesses. Homeland Security has worked out the kinks, cleaned up data, and made E-Verify more smoothly operational. E-Verify checks two sources of data; for immigrants, the immigration records Homeland Security is responsible for, and for U.S. citizens, Social Security data which the Social Security Administration is responsible for. Some technical workarounds have helped to get things fixed in a timely manner, and Homeland Security is working on both of the data component issues. On the Social Security side, the Homeland Security Department has put out regulations that deal with the no-match letter process (8 C.F.R. Part 274a [DHS Docket No. ICEB–2006–0004; ICE 2377–06] [RIN 1653–AA50]).

These were delayed by a federal judge in California in the fall of 2007. Federal Judge Charles Breyer of the Northern District of California issued a preliminary injunction putting a DHS enclosure to accompany SSA "no-match" letters on hold (*AFL-CIO v Chertoff*, NDCal, No 3:07-cv-04472-CRB). But "no-match" letters have been sent for several years, and that process will likely go forward. However, the Social Security Administration has not sent these letters for the 2006 or 2007 tax years, all relating to DHS regulatory matters pertaining to its insert. The Social Security bureaucracy will likely wait until the Homeland Security regulation dispute is settled before reinstituting "no-match" letters.

The states are enacting laws that mandate electronic employment verification. Some have mandated participation in the E-Verify program by various of their own entities and businesses in their jurisdictions. From their viewpoint, it is a way to protect the law-abiding businesses and legally eligible workers, to help ensure fair wages and working conditions, and drive out the illegal element from the community. The states have many things in mind for doing that. This approach is often referred to as shutting down the jobs magnet, and states as well as the federal government are stepping up in trying to do that. As long as it is voluntary at the federal level, then it makes complete sense that states and localities act on their legitimate responsibility to protect their citizens and the public safety of their community. This is one element of doing that, and it gives people the ability to do what we learned as American history students, that local government is the one that steps up and fashions the specific remedy for the specific problem in each locality. If it is not viewed as a problem in San Francisco but viewed as a problem in Missouri, then that is fine under our federated system for different approaches to deal with each challenge faced in the public sphere.

Health Care

A growing issue in the health care arena, relating to immigration, is uncompensated care and increasing numbers of people without health insurance. Connected here is the issue, particularly at the local level of a given clinic or hospital, of a zero sum game. There is a zero sum depletion of medical resources, whether we think in terms of a doctor or other providers' time and energy, or number of beds, bandages, and X-ray machines. Zero sum means, essentially, that there is a finite amount of something. The economy may grow, so the pie gets bigger and all who work hard and contribute benefit from having a relatively bigger piece of the pie. But in a zero-sum situation, the size of the pie doesn't grow. So when one person receives a medical service or commodity, then someone else with the same need may have to go without. Zero sum in the health care context means a finite amount of medical resources must be allocated, and when those resources are depleted, they are gone. Someone may have to go without. There is a zero-sum aspect there where immigration and health care overlap, and uncompensated care and growth in the number of uninsured relate to that. Sadly, much of the growth in these two phenomena is due to current immigration policy.

Emergency rooms, clinics, and hospitals are the real frontline places, receiving patients to whom they give uncompensated care and who are uninsured. The Emergency Medical Treatment and Labor Act (EMTALA), 42 U.S.C. § 1395dd, requires the treatment of whoever presents at a hospital emergency room, if the hospital is public or receives certain federal funds. Immigration is responsible in large part for the growth of the uninsured population. Some 71 percent of the growth in the uninsured since 1989 is due to immigration, based on census figures. Immigration adds to the number of people seeking treatment without insurance, and more people, whether they are immigrants or not, add to the congestion of the hospital or clinic. This could delay treatment of others who may be more severely ill. It complicates triage. It requires usage of equipment, devoting facilities and supplies to someone who has no legitimate reason for being in the country or no permission to be here. It could mean taking away resources to treat someone who is unlawfully present while being unable to treat someone else who is a native-born, insured citizen.

Another aspect of the problem is cost-shifting, which is something providers have to do every day to try to make ends meet in the face of growing uninsured populations and a growing level of their care being uncompensated. Other entities affected are employers, taxpayers, insurers, and government payers, meaning the financing side. Health care dollars must cover more, and cover more people, including millions of uninsured immigrants. Employers, taxpayers, insurers, and government payers are affected because most Americans get their health insurance through their employment. These payers are being stressed economically or financially, which contributes to health care's financial woes, and ranges from the local level to the state and federal health care budgets. This has serious implications for Medicare, Medicaid, and other public programs, as well as private insurance.

Another health issue is the reintroduction of diseases that can become public health threats. Deplorable things that we once eradicated are returning by way of immigration, so that is a great concern. The reintroduction of diseases such as tuberculosis and leprosy places the general public at risk because of the freedom of movement within the country. We could encounter someone carrying a disease in places we would never expect to be at risk. This forces the spending of scarce health care dollars to combat health threats that we had eradicated. This involves agencies such as the Centers for Disease Control and Prevention, and local medical facilities and providers, giving rise to allocation of resources that would otherwise be unnecessary if we were more diligent in the health screening of would be immigrants and serious about ending illegal immigration.

Attorneys can help with these health care issues by providing assistance on the front end to ensure that immigrants abide by the health provisions of the Immigration and Nationality Act (Section 212(a)(1)). We currently have on the books laws that prohibit the admission of people who carry communicable diseases, and the requirements for health screening of prospective immigrants. There is a lot of fraud in the screening process. To the extent that immigration lawyers would step up and actually help people to comply scrupulously with the law, get their own screening and submit their own results, such as X-rays, to show they do not carry active TB or other disease. Lawyers need to dissuade people from buying a clean X-ray off the street and, as officers of the court, owe the public a duty to curb fraud. It could mean the lawyer would be playing the tough love role in some instances, but the public interest has to be served, and everybody, including lawyers, owes that duty as a citizen.

Looking Ahead

The prospects of comprehensive immigration reform are increasingly doubtful, because that approach of legislation failed twice in major efforts in the Senate in 2006 and 2007, despite the White House strongly pushing the legislation and powerful special interests advocating on behalf of it. If comprehensive immigration reform legislation *were* to pass, it would quickly backfire. We would see overwhelming numbers of amnesty seekers. In 1986, that amnesty was considered extremely large, with about 3 million people legalized under that program. At this point, we are talking about an estimated 12 to 20 million illegal aliens present in the country, so it is a far larger group of potential recipients. We could anticipate newly arrived illegals among them, meaning amnesty would prompt a run to the border for those who see it as their chance to get in. You would have a large number of people who just got here as illegals who would seek the legal status the amnesty processing would accord them. Judging by the IRCA experience and the process as described in the 2006 and 2007 legislation, fraud would abound—and succeed. Therefore, any legalization program ought to be only as a "mopping up" process for the most justifiable cases, such as illegals with U.S. citizen children, who have lived in this nation for decades, have established real legitimate ties into the community and nation, who truly repent of their ways and can show that they really have Americanized and will give up their foreign ties, both formal and informal. This would follow a concerted effort to drive from this nation as many illegal aliens as possible—the vast majority of them—and real verifiable results have been achieved on the enforcement side, at the border, in the interior, in the workplace, involving law enforcement officers at every level. Any future legalization process must strengthen the requirements to obtain legal status. There were many loopholes and laxness in every recently proposed amnesty legislation, allowing people to attest for their friend that someone had been here since the requisite date. There were very lax documentation requirements, so I think there would be a lot of fraud occurring. The standards to which illegal aliens would be held for obtaining legal status that were in the U.S. Senate bills, other amnesty legislation, and discussed in Washington circles are wholly unacceptable and a recipe for disaster.

With "comprehensive immigration reform," the immigration bureaucracy would be completely swamped, unable to process all the millions of people. There would be massive fraud, all effectively leading to rubber-stamping by the government and pretty much all comers getting approved (even if they just yesterday stepped across the border). There would be a falling off of enforcement efforts because federal resources would be drained and renewed waves of immigration, both legal and illegal. The message would be sent loud and clear: The U.S. said no more amnesty, and they just passed a mega amnesty, so we will migrate illegally and then wait our turn because they will probably do it again. That would be the signal sent by "comprehensive immigration reform." If the bill were to increase legal immigration levels, then there would be an even greater inflow of immigrants. Depending on the specifics of the legislation, it might go from around 1.2 million per year to something like 2 to 4 million legal immigrants per year, because there has been little effort to change the preference system by which extended family members enter (known as chain migration). A great rise in the number of legal immigrants would spark a backlash among overwhelmed Americans.

Efforts would redouble on the state and local levels to deal with the fallout of that huge level of immigration. More crowded hospitals and schools would feel overwhelming. There could be a rise in vigilantism. Some people would take the law in their own hands, feeling their federal government sold them out, with no next step to take except to defend themselves. Amnesty and rising immigration levels could lead to strong grassroots efforts and an electoral push to reverse the tide and throw the bums out of Washington who perpetrated this massive increase in immigration on the country. Virtually every legitimate poll has consistently shown overwhelming majorities of the public opposed to amnesty, opposed to increasing legal immigration, with only a small minority supporting these policies. If the small minority wins, that leads the rest of the electorate to be motivated to take action.

On the policy front, what are most possible are incremental steps. Congress recently has been passing a few targeted immigration bills. For instance, one deals with nurses, allowing an increase in foreign nurses. Most people are not as concerned about such a targeted, temporary increase when they understand there is a nursing shortage. There are many reasons for that unrelated to immigration, such as a dearth of nursing faculty. This is because nursing requires extra education, yet one will make less money as a nursing faculty member than as a practitioner. People will generally go where they can make more money, so that pay disparity has exacerbated the situation and has nothing to do with immigration. Immigration is being used as a short-term stopgap. This is an example of the kind of limited immigration bills that might be passed. More likely are incremental steps, on the enforcement side as well, such as the bill called the Secure America through Verification and Enforcement Act, or SAVE Act (H.R. 4088, S. 2366, S. 2368). Its core provision is to phase in mandatory participation in the E-Verify program. I think those smaller, targeted incremental steps are the most feasible to actually pass.

The incremental approach does have negative aspects. One is that it leaves open loopholes that unscrupulous people will run to exploit. So where the problem is document fraud or smuggling, you could see a rise in document fraud or various aspects of smuggling. The judgment call is, given the options, is it an acceptable downside, as opposed to the large-scale harm that would be imposed by the comprehensive immigration reform route. To my mind, the lesser risks from addressing immigration challenges incrementally would be much more acceptable.

Another detrimental side to the incremental approach lies in the American people who would be unable to obtain jobs in certain sectors in the meantime. If we pass nursing visas or increase H2B visas for unskilled foreign workers in the non-agriculture sector—there has been a number of pushes for that every year for the past five years—that continues to harm the ability of American teenagers, the lowest skilled Americans, even legal immigrants without a high level of skills to obtain a job. Research by Paul Harrington, George Borjas, and others strongly indicates that immigrant labor of this sort displaces the ability of American teens to get those basic entry-level jobs, summer jobs that teach people the kind of basic skills such as showing up on time consistently, following directions, obeying the practices and policies of the workplace, learning safety risks and habits, and the order in which to do the steps of a process. Learning the realities of how changes in the market affect real-life workers, and having to deal with a supervisor who is not the most congenial person and still follow his instructions, is something we should want the next generation to learn to do in youth, and then apply those life lessons responsibly the rest of their lives. I think it should be considered one of the detriments of liberal immigration policies, incremental or comprehensive, if we deprive our native-born children of those kinds of lessons in character building.

Law enforcement agencies and prosecutors can prepare for whatever federal legislation comes by taking advantage of the federal training and resources presently available. For instance, the Justice Department has funded a state and local pilot project called the Basic Immigration Enforcement Training Program. Delivered online, it offers basic information to help local police officers apply the principles they would need if they encounter an immigrant during routine police duties. The Law Enforcement Support Center is Homeland Security's answer to provide 24/7 help to screen aliens in custody or detained by law enforcement. The Criminal Alien Program is a derivative of what was formerly called the Institutional Removal Program. If a foreign-born inmate is in custody behind bars, CAP helps to identify that person and see if he is removable—that is, if he meets the criteria for deportation. Removal and deportation are synonyms for the same concept.

Another available resource is to get ICE to start a multi-agency task force in your area. ICE at Homeland Security stands for Immigration and Customs Enforcement. Most prosecutors and law enforcement know there is a lot of interaction and cross-over between gang activity, drugs, human trafficking, other smuggling and document fraud, etc. If you ask for a multi-agency task force working with the ICE office in the locality, that can help to bring together the various law enforcement agencies in a given jurisdiction to address these problems. There are immigration connections with many of those criminal activities, especially human trafficking, drugs, and smuggling.

There is also the 287(g) program (Section 287(g) of the Immigration and Nationality Act). Also started in 1996, this program effectively provides for deputization of local or state law officers for federal immigration enforcement. A state or locality requests a memorandum of understanding with ICE, a number of local police officers receive full-fledged immigration training, and those officers interact with ICE in such things as special initiatives, investigations, prisoner screening, and initiating removal proceedings. ICE has received a growing number of requests for 287(g) arrangements. The agency has helped state and local agencies to consider which options like the CAP or task force route might be best suited to local needs. If a locality still thinks 287(g) is its best bet, officials should find an expert to help to facilitate organizing political support on Capitol Hill. Most of the state or local agencies that participate in 287(g) involved congressional allies to obtain the quickest turnaround and approval, especially when it seemed the request was going to be disapproved.

One goal of actively pursuing these resources is to gain sophistication in the immigrant enforcement policy areas. For example, gaining some training can help improve decision making and improve the ability to work with the federal authorities, and that can be beneficial. One goal would be to save taxpayers money by placing criminal aliens into federal hands as soon as possible, and thereby save state or local taxpayer dollars. Another goal would be to improve the quality of life in the community with increasingly consistent local enforcement against illegal and criminal aliens. Rudy Giuliani was famous for the "broken windows" policing in New York, rigorously going after small ticket crimes like loitering and jumping over turnstiles at the subway. Going after people who commit fairly small crimes leads to benefits of fewer infractions of a more serious nature. That is a goal of this routine immigration enforcement at the state and local level. It can help drive attrition, people deporting themselves—and that has the great benefit of improving the quality of life and public safety in your own communities.

Another objective and benefit would be to cause the disruption of criminal enterprises. If you can break up an ID fraud ring by removing its leader on immigration charges, you have disrupted that criminal enterprise or human trafficking ring or gang activities, because of the inter-connectivity among the perpetrators. If you lack evidence to prosecute on a drug or gang violation, then why not nab them on a felony for having re-entered the country after deportation? Work with your U.S. Attorney on that. It has the same benefit of getting the criminal alien off the street and protecting the community, so there are many goals, objectives, and potential benefits from this approach.

I think it all comes back to preparing for whatever federal legislation comes down the pike. Law enforcement must learn about the inherent legal authority they already have in areas related to immigration, and how to exercise it. Many areas are solely federal, such as deciding how many immigrants may come into the country, but many more areas are within the realm of inherent authority. I would encourage the exploration and exercise of that inherent authority.

James R. Edwards Jr. is a principal of the Washington consulting firm The MITA Group. On Capitol Hill, Dr. Edwards served as U.S. Rep. Ed Bryant's legislative director. He also worked for U.S. Rep. Jimmy Duncan and U.S. Sen. Strom Thurmond. Dr. Edwards co-authored The Congressional Politics of Immigration Reform. *He's an adjunct fellow with the Hudson Institute and holds degrees from the University of Georgia and the University of Tennessee.*

Considering Problematic Issues and Potential Solutions

Daniel Stein

President

Federation for American Immigration Reform

ASPATORE

Immigration

Immigration continues to be a major political issue in the United States. The two major parties have failed to address the core issue of most concern to Americans: How to make our overall immigration policy more responsive to the needs and priorities of the American people as a whole? A range of border and interior control strategies that were proposed in the first session of the 110th Congress did not appear adequate to do the job, while the amnesty, or so-called "legalization" provisions, appeared to cause far more administrative overload than the bill's sponsors were willing to admit. In 2008, there were sustained efforts to revive the political momentum behind bills that failed in 2007, while simultaneously enacting piecemeal special interest measures designed to add more visas and accelerate backlogs.

The main driving force is the disconnect between the needs of the U.S. in the twenty-first century and an immigration policy more appropriate to the nineteenth century. The U.S. is a mature state in need of immigration only for narrowly tailored applications appropriate for a post-industrial information-based superpower. Instead, we are importing millions of poorly educated, low-skill immigrants as if this were the dawn of the Industrial Revolution.

FAIR would like to revive legislation that will ensure integrity is restored to the immigration process first and foremost, while advancing legislation that will eliminate the core elements of extended family (or so called "chain") migration that have contributed to today's unmanageable backlogs and ever-increasing numbers. We have identified these issues because of our full-time study of the immigration phenomenon. The Census Bureau's periodic "Current Population Survey" is indispensable, as are periodic reports issued by the Government Accountability Office. In addition, local activists and organizations across the nation provide information on local challenges for our consideration.

The issues I face are broader than those faced by immigration officers, prosecutors, or attorneys. We wonder when this nation will have an immigration policy discussion that considers the long-range impact of adding perhaps 100 million more people to the U.S. population in the next three or four decades. How can we best determine the purposes of immigration in the twenty-first century to fashion a system and policy that meets our *domestic* priorities? In my view, the level of immigration is far too high to sustain and is already producing a wide range of structural, environmental, and social issues that were neither planned nor foreseen.

Post 9-11, the emphasis continues to center on national security and ways to ensure that intending immigrants follow the law. Moreover, there is growing public sentiment demanding reduced overall immigration and a sustained effort to halt illegal immigration. There is a wide range of reasons for this. In terms of national security, you cannot stop terrorism if you cannot control immigration. More broadly, there is growing wage and financial pressure brought on by outsourcing, increased foreign labor supplies, and a changing economic climate that forces American families to recognize the increased competition for services, jobs, and resources.

We are working hard to provide legal assistance to U.S. citizens who are discriminated against by employers who work with recruiters to hire illegal workers at reduced wages. We are also seeking methods by which lawful residents can sustain legal action to defend state and local initiatives that increase state-local cooperation with federal authorities in immigration enforcement.

On these emerging issues, we interact mostly with American citizens and legal residents adversely affected by illegal immigration. From my vantage point, the priority issue for the illegal alien advocacy groups seems to be how to gain various benefits more quickly, in the highest amounts and for the greatest number of illegals. Many permanent resident aliens and naturalized citizens are discouraged by the fact that this nation treats the rule of law so casually in the immigration context. They are proud of their achievements in scrupulously following the proper immigration process, and they feel diminished by the willingness of so many in authority positions to bend the rules for those who have blatantly broken the law multiple times.

The greatest concern of illegal immigrants is avoiding apprehension, deportation, and removal before—they believe—Congress might enact legislation granting relief from past law violations. Many illegal immigrants have worked in what are, at present, depressed industries where jobs are scarce. Encouraging an orderly return home should be top priority, not continuing to fuel unrealistic expectations about eventual citizenship.

Employment

State and local agencies are beginning to take a more active role in assisting employers in complying with their obligations to screen workers for legal status. Rather than obstructing progress in this area, employers' representatives, such as the U.S. Chamber of Commerce, should have been working diligently to help set up a reliable, low-cost method of helping employers determine work authorization for new hires. Some states are beginning to mandate that employers participate in "E-Verify," the government's pilot program set up to enable employers to verify work eligibility. Other states are testing innovative concepts that would revoke a business license for pattern and practice repeat offenders. Clearly, states are trying to find ways to increase risks for those employers who intentionally and willfully hire illegal workers as a way to reduce labor costs.

States are passing a variety of new initiatives and laws that test the limits of state action in this area. Oklahoma and Arizona have passed strong measures. In Oklahoma, a bill enacted recently makes it a crime to move, transport, or try to transport known illegal immigrants within the state. It also makes it a crime to conceal, harbor, or shelter illegal immigrants; it tightens eligibility for state driver's licenses and identity cards. The bill requires all public employers, including contractors and subcontractors, to verify work authorization of all new employees starting July 1, 2008 (although it does not require the use of E-Verify, and this provision is currently under legal challenge). Moreover, it would be considered as unlawful discrimination for an employer to discharge a legal resident while retaining an illegal immigrant hired after July 1, 2008, in a comparable job, so long as the employer knew or reasonably should have known the retained employee was illegally in this country (this provision is also subject to legal challenge). And finally, the new law requires state and local agencies to verify lawful presence for state and local public benefits, but provides exceptions for certain emergency and humanitarian services. This legislation is viewed as a model for the rest of the country.

How much latitude states possess in the field of employer sanctions and related regulation remains an open question. Congress possesses plenary power in the field of immigration regulation; therefore, changes made at the federal level could pre-empt state efforts to supplement federal enforcement initiatives. Hopefully, federal changes will increase the consequences faced by those who break the immigration laws of the United States. This can only be done by increasing the deterrence value inherent in consequences for circumventing immigration limits. Recent federal legislation such as the REAL ID Act is an effort to shore up the integrity of the nation's federalized system of driver's licenses, through such measures as limiting the issuance of driver's licenses to persons who can demonstrate legal presence in the country. Requiring states to be full partners in the field of immigration law enforcement should be a condition precedent to any discussion about blanket amnesty legislation.

State and local governments must first and foremost recognize that the days when a state official could simply shrug and say, "Immigration is a federal matter, it is not my job," are ending. States and local governments can and must be full partners in ensuring all regulations and practices are consistent with the federal scheme. This means that states can no longer be viewed as "safe harbors," providing benefits to individuals without verifying status and eligibility. It means assisting in the enforcement of immigration laws by working cooperatively with the Department of Homeland Security to ensure that aliens residing here illegally are identified and turned over to proper federal authorities. States also need to take a larger role in advising the federal government beforehand of the cost and consequences of mass immigration—and these findings should be part of the deliberative process in Congress in establishing aggregate annual levels of immigration for the nation as a whole.

Education

One of the biggest complications that arise from educating undocumented aliens comes from the fact that the Supreme Court dictated that states must provide public education at taxpayers' expense, but provided no obvious means of funding it. States cannot, by definition, plan for the increase in school-age children caused by illegal immigration. Therefore, resources will invariably have to be taken from other worthy programs and goals in order to provide education to persons who have no right to be in the country. The result? We have overcrowded and under-funded schools that impair the learning opportunities for all students.

States have construed the Supreme Court's decision in *Plyler v. Doe* (1982) to mean that they have no constitutional means of ascertaining a child's immigration status on enrollment. This is incorrect. The Supreme Court merely stated that so long as they were here, the state had an obligation to enroll the children. It did not say that states or counties were obligated to provide the benefits, no questions asked. States do not ascertain immigration status on enrollment: this not only provides one of many magnets that draws illegal immigrants to the U.S., but it also makes it nearly impossible for local taxpayers to understand the full fiscal burdens presented by continued illegal immigration.

Legal

Since 9-11, states have made varied and inconsistent efforts to bring their driver's licenses into line with various security standards. Federal law changes have now established minimum requirements in order to render states' documents valid for defined federal purposes (such as boarding a plane). These standards were spelled out in the REAL ID Act. A number of states have resisted the congressionally mandated timetable, but over time, there will have to be a full-scale verification of eligible immigration status before a driver's license is issued. Most states now require proof of either citizenship or lawful residence prior to issuing a driver's license.

There continues to be a debate about whether allowing illegal aliens to possess a driver's license contributes to, or threatens, public safety. Beyond that, there is interest in developing a scheme whereby the driver's license will no longer be valid when a non-immigrant's visa expires. We would like to see every state establish procedures to ensure that every alien who receives a driver's license must first demonstrate a legal right to be in the country.

What the Future Holds

At present, there is an impasse brought on, in my view, by the failure of amnesty proponents to grasp that the American people will not accept policy prescriptions that have proven ineffective in the past: The Immigration Reform and Control Act of 1986 delivered a massive illegal alien amnesty, in exchange for which the American people were promised that the flow of illegal immigration would be staunched through the strict enforcement of employer sanctions. That promise was never fulfilled. Instead, illegal immigration actually increased dramatically in anticipation that the "one-time only" amnesty would eventually be repeated and in the certain knowledge that employer sanctions were being enforced only in the most lackadaisical and spotty manner.

Although there are inevitable changes in the make-up of Congress over time, the fact is the American people are engaged in this issue in ways unthinkable before both 9-11 and the Internet age. My sense is that the public will not accept empty promises of future enforcement in exchange for "amnesty" programs now, not after the experience with the 1986 legislation.

Immigration is running at all-time highs. By any definition, the U.S. is undergoing sustained rates of immigration unprecedented in American history. Annual immigration rates now run over 1 million and could grow to 2 million per year, based on current trends. These rates fuel rapid population growth, which in turn affects all aspects of the nation's infrastructure and quality of life. The results are apparent everywhere, from overcrowded highways, schools, hospitals, housing, etc., and the costs of providing services for large numbers of immigrants whose educational levels do not provide the income earning ability to lift them out of poverty-level living standards. There is a general sense in this country that immigration—while fine in theory—has exceeded reasonable levels and that the government has *very* lax control over the process. There is also the a very real sense that the asylum and deportation processes are subject to manipulation and abuse routinely.

States will need to become full partners in the enhancements required to make interior immigration enforcement effective. Public demands for apprehension, detention, and removal will only grow as the economic framework of the U.S. shifts in response to a global trading system that sharply reduces the U.S. need for unskilled and semi-skilled labor.

Daniel Stein is the president of FAIR, the Federation for American Immigration Reform, the nation's largest national membership organization dedicated to immigration policy, with 198,000 members and supporters.

Mr. Stein is one of the nation's most frequently cited experts on U.S. immigration policy. He has testified more than fifty times before Congress, and regularly appears as a guest on national network television. He has been featured on every major national news program in America, including 60 Minutes, This Week, *and* Face the Nation.

Mr. Stein has directed FAIR since 1988—as executive director from 1988 to 2004, and president since. Prior to 1988, he served as executive director of the Immigration Reform Law Institute (IRLI), where he was involved in a variety of federal administrative law cases pertaining to U.S. immigration controls. From 1977 to 1982, Mr. Stein served as a professional staff member of the U.S. House of Representatives House Select Committee on Narcotics Abuse and Control.

Mr. Stein is an attorney licensed in Washington D.C. and Maryland. He is a graduate of Indiana University (economics) and Columbus School of Law. He is a native of Washington, D.C.

Appendices

Appendix A

ADMINISTRATION FOR CHILDREN AND FAMILIES

OFFICE OF REFUGEE RESETTLEMENT

STATE LETTER: #00-17

Purpose of this Letter

This State Letter outlines: (1) the statuses that confer eligibility for Refugee Resettlement Program benefits; (2) the documentation that is needed to prove an individual has one of those statuses; and (3) a suggested process for making eligibility determinations. Along with confirming status, eligibility determinations must include confirmation of identity, the date that an individual initially became eligible for benefits ("entry" date) and, in cases involving Cuban and Haitian entrants, nationality. More than one piece of documentation may be needed to make all of these determinations. **However, this State Letter will not discuss documentation that confirms identity, nationality or "entry" dates. This State Letter only discusses status documentation.**

Process

The Office of Refugee Resettlement (ORR) asks agencies to use the following process when determining eligibility for Refugee Resettlement Program benefits.

(1) Eligibility workers should ask the applicant for a **written declaration**, under penalty of perjury, that he or she has an immigration status that makes him or her eligible for Refugee Resettlement Program benefits.

(2) Eligibility workers should review **documentation** of immigration status as outlined in charts included with this State Letter.

(3) If status is supported by documents, eligibility workers may conclude that the applicant has a qualified status and continue with **other eligibility verifications**, such as verification of "entry date" and specific program requirements.

(4) If unable to confirm status after checking documentation, which suggests eligibility, agencies should provide benefits while using **other**

methods to verify status. Agencies, if connected with the Immigration and Naturalization Service (INS) Systematic Alien Verification for Entitlements (SAVE) system should follow standard SAVE procedures. If not connected to the SAVE system, agencies may submit INS Form G-845 to the local INS office. In some cases, which are mentioned below, agencies may call the Executive Office for Immigration Review (EOIR) case status line.

(5) If an agency follows the above procedures but remains uncertain about an applicant's status, please call AnnaMarie Bena, **ORR Immigration Specialist**, at (202) 260-5186 or send an email to abena@acf.dhhs.gov.

Limitations

ORR has attempted to gather a comprehensive list of documents that shows statuses conferring eligibility for ORR programs. However, the INS produces a variety of documents, some of which may be useful in a status determination but which, for a number of reasons, may not have been included in this State Letter. Moreover, due to the complexity of certain categorical definitions, documentation alone may not definitively confirm eligibility in some cases. Noting these difficulties, ORR asks agencies to follow the process suggested above. If an agency has concerns or questions at any point during the process, please contact Anna Marie Bena at (202) 260-5186 or abena@acf.dhhs.gov.

Proposed Rule

In August 1998, the Attorney General published a proposed rule, ***Verification of Eligibility for Public Benefits***, 63 FR 41662, ("Proposed Rule"), with a 60-day comment period. The Proposed Rule is not in force. However, the Attorney General is expected to issue a final rule concerning verification issues. At that time, ORR will reevaluate the guidance in this letter to ensure that ORR procedures are consistent with the final verification rules. Agencies should follow the guidance in this State Letter until a final rule is issued by the Attorney General.

STATUS REQUIREMENTS

Individuals with the following statuses are eligible for Refugee Resettlement Program benefits (45 CFR §400.43(a)(1)-(6)):

1. the Immigration and Nationality Act (INA)
2. Refugees admitted under §207 of the INA
3. Asylees whose status was granted under §208 of the INA
4. Individuals paroled as **refugees or asylees** under §212(d)(5) of Cuban and Haitian entrants, in accordance with the requirements in 45 CFR §401.2

    a. Any individual granted parole status as a Cuban/Haitian Entrant (Status Pending) or granted any other special status subsequently established under the immigration laws for nationals of Cuba or Haiti, regardless of the status of the individual at the time assistance or services are provided

    b. A national of Cuba or Haiti who was paroled into the United States and has not acquired any other status under the INA and with respect to whom a final, nonappealable, and legally enforceable order of removal, deportation or exclusion has not been entered

    c. A national of Cuba or Haiti who is the subject of removal, deportation or exclusion proceedings under the INA and with respect to whom a final, nonappealable, and legally enforceable order of removal, deportation or exclusion has not been entered

    d. A national of Cuba or Haiti who has an application for asylum pending with the INS and with respect to whom a final, nonappealable, and legally enforceable order of removal, deportation or exclusion has not been entered

5. Certain Amerasians from Vietnam who are admitted to the U.S. as immigrants pursuant to §584 of the Foreign Operations, Export Financing, and Related Programs Appropriations Act, 1988 (as contained in §101(e) of Public Law 100-202 and amended by the 9th proviso under Migration and Refugee Assistance in title II of the Foreign Operations, Export Financing, and Related Programs Appropriations Acts, 1989 (Public Law 100-461 as amended)
6. Lawful permanent residents, provided the individuals previously held one of the statuses identified above (Note that this does not refer to

Amerasians who are admitted as lawful permanent residents. See #5 above.)

DOCUMENTATION REQUIREMENTS

In order to access Refugee Resettlement program benefits, individuals must provide acceptable documentation of one of the statuses listed above. The following lists include documents that provide proof of these statuses. These documents may or may not provide proof of identity, nationality or "entry" date.

Chart #1

1. **Acceptable documents for individuals paroled as refugee or asylees under §212(d)(5) of the INA*:**

Documents/Codes	Comments
I-94 Arrival/departure card noting that the individual has been paroled as a **refugee or asylee** under §212(d)(5)	To be eligible under this provision, the I-94 must note that the individual is a **refugee or asylee**.
I-766 Employment Authorization Document with the code A04	
I-688B Employment Authorization Document with the provision of law 274a.12(a)(4)	This is an older version of the employment authorization document but it is still in use.

***Note**: This status rarely has been granted since 1980. **It is unlikely that eligibility workers will encounter this type of documentation.** Eligibility workers may encounter other individuals, not refugees or asylees, who have been paroled under §212(d)(5). The documentation of other parolees under §212(d)(5) may include language, such as "humanitarian" or "public interest parole." An example of a population with this documentation would be parolees who receive benefits under the "Lautenberg Amendment," a special provision that allows nationals from the former Soviet Union, Vietnam, Laos or Cambodia to adjust their status after having resided in the United States for one year. These types of parolees under §212(d)(5) are NOT eligible for ORR benefits. Only individuals who are listed as **refugees or asylees** are eligible under this provision. However, if the individual is a national of Cuba or Haiti, he or she may be eligible under the provisions concerning Cuban and Haitian entrants. (See documentation lists below for information on Cuban and Haitian entrants.)

Chart #2

2. **Acceptable documents for refugees admitted under §207 of the INA:**

Documents/Codes	Comments
I-94 Arrival/departure card noting that the individual has been admitted under §207 of the INA	Notations may include references to employment authorization, indefinite status, and the requirement to obtain permission before leaving the United States.
RE-1 admission code on the I-94	Principal Refugee
RE-2 admission code on the I-94	Spouse of principal refugee
RE-3 admission code on the I-94	Child of principal refugee
RE-4 admission code on the I-94	Collateral relatives of principal refugee
RE-5 admission code on the I-94	Certain Haitian refugees
I-766 Employment Authorization Document with the code A03	
I-688B Employment	This is an older version of the

Authorization Document with the provision of law 274a.12(a)(3)	employment authorization document but it is still in use.
INS Form I-571	U.S. Refugee Travel Document*
Visa 93 (or V-93) on the I-94 Arrival/departure card	May be accompanied by the words "section 207"; Individual is the spouse or minor child of a previously admitted refugee.

***Note**: The INS Form I-571, which is a United States Refugee Travel Document, does not distinguish between refugees and asylees. An individual with a United States Refugee Travel Document may be a refugee or an asylee.

Chart #3

3. **Acceptable documents for asylees whose status was granted under §208 of the INA:**

Documents/Codes	**Comments**
I-94 Arrival/departure card noting that the individual has been admitted under §207 of the INA	Notations may include references to employment authorization, indefinite status, and the requirement to obtain permission before leaving the United States.
AS-1 admission code on the I-94	Approved asylee principal
AS-2 admission code on the I-94	Approved spouse of an asylee principal

AS-3 admission code on the I-94	Approved child of an asylee principal
INS Form I-571	United States Refugee Travel Document*
I-766 Employment Authorization Document with the code A05	
I-688B Employment Authorization Document with the provision of law 274a.12(a)(5)	This is an older version of the employment authorization document but it is still in use.
Order of an Immigration Judge ranting Asylum under §208 of the INA	An Order of an Immigration Judge will serve as proof of asylee status if the INS has waived the right to appeal the case. See Note 2 below for information about cases where the INS reserves the right to appeal.**
Asylum Approval Letter from an INS Asylum Office	Letter will note that the individual has been granted asylum pursuant to §208 of the INA and may include information concerning refugee and asylee relative petition, work authorization and the refugee travel document.

Written decision from the Board of Immigration Appeals (BIA)	
I-730 Approval Letter	The I-730 Approval Letter may be used as proof of asylee status for derivatives.
Visa 92 (or V-92) on the I-94 Arrival/departure card	May be accompanied by the words "section 208"; Individual is the spouse or minor child of a previously granted asylee.

***Note 1**: The INS Form I-571, which is a United States Refugee Travel Document, does not distinguish between refugees and asylees. An individual with a United States Refugee Travel Document may be a refugee or an asylee.

****Note 2:** If the INS has reserved its right to appeal, an Immigration Judge Order will not serve, on its own, as proof of asylee status. If an asylee brings an Immigration Judge Order that shows the INS has reserved its right to appeal, eligibility workers must wait 30 days from the date on the Immigration Judge Order. On or after the 31st day, the eligibility worker will need to call the Executive Office for Immigration Review (EOIR) case status line at (800) 898-7180 to find out whether the INS has appealed the case. (The EOIR reports that it may take up to 5 days after the appeal deadline for the information to be relayed to the case status line.) If the INS has appealed the case, the individual is not yet an asylee and is not eligible for benefits. If the INS has not appealed the case and 30 days have passed since the date on the Immigration Judge Order, the individual is an asylee and is eligible for ORR assistance and services.

Chart #4a

4a. Acceptable documents for Cuban and Haitian entrants, in accordance with the requirements in 45 CFR §401.2: Any individual granted parole status as a Cuban/Haitian Entrant (Status Pending) or granted any other special status* subsequently established under the immigration laws for nationals of Cuba or Haiti, regardless of the status of the individual at the time assistance or services are provided

Documents/Codes	Comments
An I-94 Arrival/departure card with a stamp showing parole at any time as a "Cuban/Haitian Entrant (Status Pending)"	I-94 may refer to §212(d)(5)
CH6 adjustment code on the I-551	Even after a Cuban/Haitian Entrant (Status Pending) becomes a permanent resident, he/she technically retains the status Cuban/Haitian Entrant (Status Pending).
An I-94 Arrival/departure card with a stamp showing parole into the U.S. on or after April 21, 1980	I-94 may refer to §212(d)(5).
A Cuban or Haitian passport with a §212(d)(5) stamp dated after October 10, 1980.	

Note**: ORR is not interpreting the phrase, "any other special status subsequently established under the immigration laws for nationals of Cuba or Haiti" to refer to lawful permanent residence obtained under the Nicaraguan Adjustment and Central American Relief Act (NACARA) or the Haitian Refugee Immigration Fairness Act (HRIFA). Although NACARA and HRIFA offer a special opportunity for nationals of Cuba and Haiti, the ***status conferred by these laws, ***lawful permanent residence***, is not a "special status." Thus, if the person did not qualify as a Cuban and Haitian entrant, adjustment of status, regardless of the legal basis for the adjustment, does not make the person a Cuban and Haitian entrant.

Chart #4b

4b. A national of Cuba or Haiti who was paroled into the United States and has not acquired any other status under the INA and with respect to whom a final, nonappealable, and legally enforceable order of removal, deportation or exclusion* has not been entered

Documents/Codes	Comments
An I-94 Arrival/departure card showing parole into the United States	I-94 may refer to §212(d)(5), humanitarian or public interest parole.**
I-766 Employment Authorization Document with the code A04	
I-766 Employment Authorization Document with the code C11	
I-688B Employment Authorization Document with the provision of law 274a.12(a)(4)***	This is an older version of the employment authorization document but it is still in use.

I-688B Employment Authorization Document with the provision of law 274a.12(c)(11)***	This is an older version of the employment authorization document but it is still in use.

***Note 1:** The question of whether there is a final, nonappealable, legally enforceable order of removal, deportation or exclusion is essentially a legal determination that cannot simply be made by reviewing any of the listed documents. Moreover, it is not a decision that can be easily made by eligibility workers in the regular course of eligibility determinations. ORR suggests that eligibility workers require a written declaration, under penalty of perjury, that the individual has a status that makes him/her eligible for ORR programs and attempt to use other methods to uncover this information, such as calling the EOIR case status line at (800) 898-7180, submitting Form G-845 to the local INS office, asking the applicant for more information or, if participating, accessing the INS SAVE system. Note that these methods may not be definitive. If an applicant appears eligible from the available information, the agency should provide benefits while conducting further investigation. If, after reviewing documents and attempting to determine whether there is a final, nonappealable, legally enforceable order of removal, deportation or exclusion, an eligibility worker remains uncertain about an applicant's eligibility, please call Anna Marie Bena at (202) 260-5186.

****Note 2**: As treatment of Cuban and Haitian entrants has developed, INS officials, on occasion, may have used notations on the I-94s of Cuban and Haitian entrants that are not listed above. Eligibility workers may see various notations that convey parole. For example, eligibility workers, in the past, may have seen the notation, "EWI," which technically stands for "Entered Without Inspection" but was being used for individuals who were paroled. Please call Anna Marie Bena at (202) 260-5186 if you encounter unusual notations or if you are uncertain of the relevance of a particular notation.

*****Note 3**: If an individual provides an I-688B Employment Authorization Document, which does not provide information about nationality, eligibility workers must request other documentation to confirm that the individual is a Cuban or Haitian national.

<u>**Chart #4c**</u>

4c. A national of Cuba or Haiti who is the subject of removal, deportation or exclusion proceedings* under the INA and with respect to whom a final, nonappealable, and legally enforceable order of removal, deportation or exclusion has not been entered**

Documents/Codes	Comments
INS Form I-221	Order to Show Cause and Notice of Hearing
INS Form I-862	Notice to Appear
INS Form I-220A	Order of Release on Recognizance
INS Form I-122	Notice to Applicant Detained for a Hearing Before an Immigration Judge
INS Form I-221S	Order to Show Cause, Notice of Hearing and Warrant for Arrest
Copy of INS Form I-589 date stamped by the Executive Office for Immigration Review (EOIR)	Application for Asylum and Withholding of Removal; Individual is subject of removal, deportation or exclusion proceedings.
Copy of INS Form I-485 date stamped by EOIR	Application to Register Permanent Residence or to Adjust Status; Individual is subject of removal, exclusion or deportation proceedings.

EOIR-26	Notice of Appeal, date stamped by the Office of the Immigration Judge
I-766 Employment Authorization Document with the code C10	Application for suspension of deportation/cancellation of removal submitted
I-688B Employment Authorization Document with the provision of law 274a.12(c)(10)***	Application for suspension of deportation/cancellation of removal submitted
Other applications for relief that have been date stamped by EOIR	
Other documentation pertaining to an applicant's removal, exclusion or deportation proceedings	Example: a notice of a hearing date before an Immigration Judge

***Note 1**: Although the above documents show that proceedings have been initiated in a case, they cannot confirm that proceedings are continuing. In order to confirm that proceedings are continuing, eligibility workers will need to use other methods, such as calling the EOIR case status line at (800) 898-7180, submitting Form G-845 to the local INS office or, if participating, accessing the INS SAVE system. If an eligibility worker cannot determine whether proceedings are ongoing, please call Anna Marie Bena at (202) 260-5186.

****Note 2:** The question of whether there is a final, nonappealable, legally enforceable order of removal, deportation or exclusion is essentially a legal determination that cannot simply be made by reviewing any of the listed documents. Moreover, it is not a decision that can be easily made by eligibility workers in the regular course of eligibility determinations. ORR suggests that eligibility workers require a written declaration, under penalty of perjury, that the individual has a status that makes him/her eligible for ORR programs and attempt to use other methods to uncover this information, such as calling the EOIR case status line at (800) 898-7180, submitting Form G-845 to the local INS office, asking the applicant for more information or, if participating, accessing the INS SAVE system. Note that these methods may not be definitive. If an applicant appears eligible from the available information, the agency should provide benefits while conducting further investigation. If, after reviewing documents and attempting to determine whether there is a final, nonappealable, legally enforceable order of removal, deportation or exclusion, an eligibility worker remains uncertain about an applicant's eligibility, please call Anna Marie Bena at (202) 260-5186.

*****Note 3**: If an individual provides an I-688B Employment Authorization Document, which does not provide information about nationality, eligibility workers must request other documentation to confirm that the individual is a Cuban or Haitian national.

<u>Chart #4d</u>

4d. A national of Cuba or Haiti who has an application for asylum pending with the Immigration and Naturalization Service and with respect to whom a final, nonappealable, and legally enforceable order of removal, deportation or exclusion* has not been entered

Documents/Codes	Comments
INS receipt for filing Form I-589	Application for Asylum and Withholding of Removal
I-766 Employment Authorization document with the code C08	
I-688B Employment Authorization Document with the provision of law 274a.12(c)(8)**	This is an older version of the employment authorization document but it is still in use.

***Note 1:** The question of whether there is a final, nonappealable, legally enforceable order of removal, deportation or exclusion is essentially a legal determination that cannot simply be made by reviewing any of the listed documents. Moreover, it is not a decision that can be easily made by eligibility workers in the regular course of eligibility determinations. ORR suggests that eligibility workers require a written declaration, under penalty of perjury, that the individual has a status that makes him/her eligible for ORR programs and attempt to use other methods to uncover this information, such as calling the EOIR case status line at (800) 898-7180, submitting Form G-845 to the local INS office, asking the applicant for more information or, if participating, accessing the INS SAVE system. Note that these methods may not be definitive. If an applicant appears eligible from the available information, the agency should provide benefits while conducting further investigation. If, after reviewing documents and attempting to determine whether there is a final, nonappealable, legally enforceable order of removal, deportation or exclusion, an eligibility worker remains uncertain about an applicant's eligibility, please call Anna Marie Bena at (202) 260-5186.

****Note 2:** If an individual provides an I-688B Employment Authorization Document, which does not provide information about nationality, eligibility workers must request other documentation to confirm that the individual is a Cuban or Haitian national.

<u>**Chart #5**</u>

5. **Acceptable documents for certain Amerasians (see definition above):**

Documents/Codes	Comments
AM-1 admission code on the I-94	Amerasian born in Vietnam after Jan. 1, 1962 and before Jan. 1, 1976 who was fathered by a U.S. citizen
AM-2 admission code on the I-94	Spouse or child of Amerasian
AM-3 admission code on the I-94	Mother, guardian or next-of-kin of Amerasian

AM-6 adjustment code on Form I-551 Permanent Resident Card (or Resident Alien Card)	Amerasian (see above)
AM-7 adjustment code on Form I-551 Permanent Resident Card (or Resident Alien Card)	Spouse or child of Amerasian
AM-8 adjustment code on Form I-551 Permanent Resident Card (or Resident Alien Card)	Mother, guardian or next-of-kin of Amerasian
Vietnamese Exit Visa with codes AM-1, AM-2 or AM-3	"Laissez Passer"; may have temporary I-551 stamp
Vietnamese passport with codes AM-1, AM-2 or AM-3	May have temporary I-551 stamp
U. S. passport coded AM-1, AM-2 or AM-3	

<u>**Chart #6**</u>

6. **Acceptable documents for lawful permanent residents who previously held one of the above identified statuses** (Note that this does not refer to Amerasians who are admitted as lawful permanent residents. See Chart #5 for all documents pertaining to Amerasians):

Form I-551 Permanent Resident Card (or Resident Alien Card) with the following codes	**Comments**
RE 6	Adjusted Principal Refugee

RE 7	Spouse of RE6
RE 8	Child of RE 6
RE 9	Collateral Relatives of RE6
AS 6	Adjusted Principal Asylee
AS 7	Spouse of AS 6
AS 8	Child of AS 6
CH 6	Adjusted Cuban/Haitian Entrant (Status Pending)
HA 6	Adjusted Cuban and Haitian Entrant (Haitian national who had applied for asylum)
HB 6	Adjusted Cuban and Haitian Entrant (Haitian national who had been paroled)
GA 6	Adjusted Iraqi asylee
GA 7	Spouse of GA 6
GA 8	Child of GA 6

Foreign Passport with unexpired, temporary I-551 stamp and the following codes:	**Comments**
RE 6	Adjusted Principal Refugee
RE 7	Spouse of RE 6
RE 8	Child of RE 6

RE 9	Collateral Relative of RE 6
AS 6	Adjusted Principal Asylee
AS 7	Spouse of AS 6
AS 8	Child of AS 6

Employment Authorization Documents	**Comments**
Form I-766 Employment Authorization Document with the code A10 (This code only confirms eligibility for Cuban or Haitian nationals.)	Withholding of Deportation or Removal
Form I-688B Employment Authorization Document with the provision of law 274a.12(a)(10) (This code only confirms eligibility for Cuban or Haitian nationals.)	Withholding of Deportation or Removal

Courtesy of Norman Levine, New Mexico Human Services Department

Appendix B

NEW MEXICO ADMINISTRATIVE CODE REQUIREMENTS FOR NON-CITIZEN DRIVERS' LICENSE (10/1/07)

TITLE 18: TRANSPORTATION AND HIGHWAYS
CHAPTER 19: MOTOR VEHICLE PROCEDURES, LICENSES, PERMITS
PART 5: DRIVER'S LICENSE
18.19.5.12 PROOF OF IDENTIFICATION NUMBER, IDENTITY AND RESIDENCY:

A. Applicants for a New Mexico identification card, driving permit, provisional driver's license or driver's license, other than a commercial driver's license, must provide documentary proof of their identification number, identity and residency.

B. A person applying for a driver's license or identification card that was lost can use a New Mexico enhanced driver's license photo from the motor vehicle division (MVD) database as proof of identity and identification number, subject to MVD's ability to verify the applicant's social security number or other identification number used to obtain the driver's license or identification card, as sufficient proof to issue a replacement driver's license or identification card.

C. Any applicant eligible for a social security number must produce their social security card in order to provide evidence of the identification number. An applicant who cannot provide the social security card must provide two of the following documents:

(1) a United States, state, or local government-issued medical card through which the social security number can be verified;

(2) a statement from a federally regulated financial institution through which the social security number can be verified; or

(3) any document in Subsection F of this section, as long as the document can be used to verify the social security number and is not used for proof of both identification number and identity.

D. In order to prove identification number, a foreign national who is unable to obtain a social security number must produce documentary proof of a matricula consular card issued after February 1, 2005, by the Mexican consulate in Albuquerque or El Paso or an individual tax identification number (ITIN). The applicant's ITIN card or the applicant's letter from the IRS issuing the ITIN is sufficient proof of the ITIN. Foreign nationals ineligible for a matricula consular card issued after February 1, 2005, by the Mexican consulate in Albuquerque or El Paso or an ITIN must present as proof of identification number, a valid passport issued by their country of citizenship.

E. Applicants must produce one of the following documents as proof of identity:

(1) original birth certificate issued by a state or territory of the United States;

(2) certified copy of birth certificate issued by a state or territory of the United States;

(3) an original or certified copy of a foreign birth certificate with a notarized English translation;

(4) original official copy of an FS545 or FS1350 form certifying birth abroad and translated into English;

(5) affidavit of Indian birth;

(6) N560 certificate of citizenship;

(7) N550 certificate of naturalization;

(8) a valid permanent resident card issued by the United States government;

(9) a valid I-551 resident alien card issued since 1997;

(10) a court order for name change, gender change, adoption or divorce, as long as it includes the legal name, date of birth and court seal;

(11) a marriage certificate issued by a state or a territory of the United States; or

(12) any document contained in Subsection F of this section, as long as the document is not used for proof of both identification number and identity.

F. Applicants can use the following documents to provide documentary proof of their identification number or documentary proof of their identity but the document cannot be used for proof of both their identification number and identity:

(1) a state issued driver's license, a driver's license issued by a territory of the United States, or by jurisdiction of Canada, as long as it has a photograph and has not been expired more than one month;

(2) a state government-issued photo identification card, or a photo identification card issued by a territory of the United States, or by a

jurisdiction of Canada, as long as it has a photograph and has not been expired more than one month; however, the MVD photo identification document card issued by MVD pursuant to Subsection J of this section may not be used to satisfy this proof of identification number requirement;

(3) a state government-issued photo learner's permit, or a photo learner's permit issued by a territory of the United States, or by a jurisdiction of Canada, as long as it has a photograph and has not been expired more than one month;

(4) a matricula consular card issued after February 1, 2005, by the Mexican consulate in Albuquerque or El Paso;

(5) a valid passport issued by country of citizenship;

(6) an American Indian or Alaskan proof of Indian blood, certificate of degree of Indian blood, federal Indian census card or tribal membership card;

(7) a photo identification card issued by the United States military, United States coast guard or New Mexico national guard;

(8) an identification document issued by the United States veterans administration, so long as it is accompanied by a United States veterans administration medical center ID card;

(9) a valid United States active duty/retiree/reservist military identification card (DOD ID DD-2); or

(10) a United States, state, or local government-issued photo ID, issued based on name, social security number and date of birth.

G. Applicants fifteen years of age or older must provide two of the following documents, showing a New Mexico address for the applicant, as proof that the applicant lives in New Mexico:

(1) a real property rental agreement or purchase agreement;

(2) a utility bill, such as water, gas, electric, waste, telephone, cable or satellite bill, but not a bill for a cell phone;

(3) an insurance bill;

(4) a bank statement;

(5) an employment pay stub that contains the applicant's name and address;

(6) a local property tax statement or mortgage documents;

(7) proof of a minor child enrolled in a New Mexico public, private, or tribal school;

(8) a current, valid motor vehicle registration;

(9) original documents from a New Mexico community organization attesting to the fact that the applicant is a New Mexico resident;

(10) original documents from a city, county, state, tribal or federal government organization attesting to the fact that the applicant; is a New Mexico resident;

(11) a New Mexico medical assistance card; or

(12) a New Mexico public assistance card.

H. Applicants less than fifteen years of age applying for an identification card must provide one of the following documents, showing a New Mexico address for the applicant, as proof that the applicant lives in New Mexico:

(1) proof that the child is enrolled in a New Mexico public, private, or tribal school;

(2) a bank statement;

(3) an affidavit from the applicant's parent or guardian stating that the applicant lives with that person, as long as the affidavit is accompanied by the parent/guardian's New Mexico driver's license, New Mexico identification card, or two proofs of New Mexico residency;

(4) original documents from a New Mexico community organization attesting to the fact that the applicant is a New Mexico resident;

(5) original documents from a city, county, state, tribal or federal government organization attesting to the fact that the applicant is a New Mexico resident;

(6) documents from membership in a New Mexico religious organization; or

(7) documents from membership in a New Mexico sports organization.

I. MVD may require foreign nationals or first-time applicants from another state, to provide a certified copy of their driving record with an English language translation, if applicable, from the jurisdiction where the applicant is currently or was previously licensed.

J. Applicants who are unable to meet the requirements for a New Mexico identification card, driving permit, provisional driver's license, or driver's license, may apply for an MVD photo identification document card. The MVD photo identification document card issued by MVD does not necessarily meet federal identification requirements. This card will be clearly identified on the card as a restricted card that cannot be used for certain purposes. The identification document cannot be used to apply for a New Mexico identification card, driving permit, provisional driver's license or driver's license. An applicant for the MVD photo identification document card must provide two documentary proofs of their identity and one documentary proof of residency.

(1) Applicants must produce two forms of documentation with their name and date of birth or with their name and social security number. Two documents with name and date of birth or two documents with name and social security number are acceptable. Any two of the following documents containing the name and date of birth or name and social security number are acceptable to prove identity:

(a) a state issued driver's license, a driver's license issued by a territory of the United States, or a license issued by a jurisdiction of Canada, as long as it has a photograph and has not been expired more than one year;

(b) a state issued identification card, an identification card issued by a territory of the United States, or an identification card issued by a jurisdiction of Canada, as long as it has a photograph and has not been expired more than one year;

(c) a state issued photo learner's permit, a photo learner's permit issued by a territory of the United States, or a photo learner's permit issued by a jurisdiction of Canada, as long as it has a photograph and has not been expired more than one year;

(d) an original or certified copy of the birth certificate issued by a United States state or territory of the United States;

(e) an affidavit of Indian birth;

(f) a current passport issued by the United States;

(g) a valid passport issued by country of citizenship;

(h) an I-94 form presented without a passport if it contains the applicant's photo;

(i) American Indian or Alaskan proof of Indian blood, certificate of degree of Indian blood, federal Indian census card or tribal membership card;

(j) N550 United States certificate of naturalization;

(k) a certificate of citizenship (N560);

(l) a resident alien card (I-551, AR-3, AR3A, AR-103) that contains the applicant's photo;

(m) FS545 or FS1350 United States certificate of birth abroad;

(n) a military identification card that includes the applicant's photo;

(o) a United States veterans administration card that includes the applicant's photo, so long as it is accompanied by a United States veterans administration medical center identification card;

(p) a medical card that includes the applicant's photo;

(q) a military dependent identification card that includes the applicant's photo;

(r) a government-issued photo identification card;

(s) a matricula consular card issued after February 1, 2005, by the Mexican consulate in Albuquerque or El Paso;

(t) a New Mexico corrections department photo identification card with name, date of birth and documentation that the card has not expired within the past year;

(u) an infant baptismal certificate;

(v) a social security card;

(w) a bank card, debit card, or credit card that contains the applicant's photo;

(x) a high school, GED, college, trade school, or university transcript, certificate, or diploma;

(y) an employee identification badge that contains the applicant's photo;

(z) a medical insurance card or documentation of medical insurance coverage or eligibility that contains an identification number;

(aa) military discharge/separation papers (DD-214);

(bb) selective service card;

(cc) proof of eligibility for and receipt of welfare benefits;

(dd) medical records;

(ee) documentation from a federal, state, or local correctional facility; or

(ff) a social security administration benefits award letter containing the social security number.

(2) Applicants must provide one or more of the following documents, showing a New Mexico address for the applicant, as proof that the applicant lives in New Mexico:

(a) a real property rental agreement or purchase agreement;

(b) a utility bill, such as a gas, electric, waste, water, cable, satellite bill, or telephone bill but not a bill for a cell phone;

(c) an insurance bill, such as automobile, home or health;

(d) a federally regulated financial institution document, such as a bank statement, excluding checks;

(e) an employment pay stub with name and address;

(f) a local property tax statement with name and address;

(g) proof of a minor child enrolled in a New Mexico public, private, or tribal school;

(h) a current, valid motor vehicle registration;

(i) original documents from a New Mexico community organization attesting to the fact that the applicant is a New Mexico resident;

(j) original documents from a city, county, state, tribal, or federal government or social service organization attesting to the fact that the applicant is a New Mexico resident;

(k) a matricula consular card issued after February 1, 2005, by the Mexican consulate in Albuquerque or El Paso;

(l) documentation of eligibility and proof that the applicant is currently receiving services from a 501(c)(3) organization, as defined by the Internal Revenue Code; or

(m) other documents as approved by the MVD director.

K. This version of 18.19.5.12 NMAC is effective on October 1, 2007.

[18.19.5.12 NMAC - N, 6/29/01; A, 6/14/02; A, 6/30/03; A, 10/1/07]

Courtesy of Norman Levine, New Mexico Human Services Department

Appendix C

SAN FRANCISCO IMMIGRANTS RIGHTS COMMISSION COMPLIANCE CHECKLIST

Checklist		Oct. 15th Compliance Plan
	1	The number and percentage of limited English speaking persons who actually use the Department's services citywide, listed by language other than English, using the method in Section 89.2(j) of the Ordinance. **89.2(j)** Public Contact Position shall mean a position in which a primary job responsibility consists of meeting, contacting, & dealing with the public in the performance of the duties of that position.
	2	The number and percentage of p0ersons who use the services provided by a Covered Department Facility , listed by language other than English, using the method in Section 89.2(j) of the Ordinance
	3	The number of Public Contact Persons in the Department
	4	The number of Bilingual Employees in Public Contact Positions, their titles, office locations, and languages other than English that the persons speak.
	5	A description of any use of telephone-based interpretation services, including the number of times such services were used and the language(s) for which they were used.
	6	A narrative assessment of the procedures used to facilitate communication with Limited English Speaking Persons, which shall include an assessment of the adequacy of the procedures.
	7	A numerical assessment of the additional Bilingual Employees in Public Contact Positions needed to meet the requirements of Section 89.3 of the Ordinance. **89.3 Equal Access to Services (a)** Utilizing sufficient Bilingual Employees in Public Contact Positions, Departments shall provide information & swervices to the public in each language spoken by a Substantial Number of Limited English Speaking Persons or to the public served by a Covered Department Facility in each language spoken by a Concentrated Number of Limited English Speaking Persons. **(b)** Departments need only implement the hiring requirements in this Ordinance by filling Public Contact Positions made vacant by retirement or normal attrition.

		Nothing herein shall be construed to authorize the dismissal of any City employee in order to carry out this Ordinance. **(c)** This Article shall be interpreted & applied so as to be consistent with Title VII of the Civil Rights Act of 1964, California's Fair Employment & Housing Act, and Article X of the San Francisco City Charter & so as not to impede or impair the City's obligations with any court order or consent decree.
	8	If assessments indicate a need for additional Bilingual Employees in Public Contact Positions to meet the requirements of 89.3 of the Ordinance, a description of the Department's plan for filling the positions, including the number of estimated vacancies in Public Contact Positions.
	9	The name, title and language(s) other than English (if any) spoken by the staff member designated with responsibility for ensuring the accuracy and appropriateness of translations for each language in which services must be provided under Section 89.3 of the Ordinance.
		A list of the Department's written materials required to be translated under the Ordinance, the language(s) into which they have been translated, and the staff person who has reviewed the translated material for accuracy and appropriateness.
	10	A description of the Department's procedures for accepting and resolving complaints of an alleged violation of the Ordinance.
	11	A copy of written policies on providing services to Limited English Speaking Persons.
	12	A list of goals for the upcoming year.
	13	Any other information requested by the Commission necessary for the implementation of the Ordinance.

Courtesy of Norman Levine, New Mexico Human Services Department

Appendix D

TESTIMONY OF KRIS KOBACH ON THE CLEAR ACT

Kris W. Kobach
Legislative Hearing on H.R. 2671, the "Clear Law Enforcement for Criminal Alien Removal Act of 2003" (CLEAR Act).

TESTIMONY OF KRIS W. KOBACH

PROFESSOR OF LAW, UNIVERSITY OF MISSOURI-KANSAS CITY

OCTOBER 1, 2003

State and Local Authority to Enforce Immigration Law AND A REVIEW OF THE PROPOSED CLEAR ACT.

The terrorist attacks of September 11, 2001, underscored for all Americans the need to restore the rule of law in the immigration arena. Terrorists were able to enter the country undetected, overstay their visas with impunity, and move freely within the country without interference from local law enforcement officers. Each of these realities created a vulnerability that the hijackers of September 11 exploited.

Enforcing our nation's immigration laws is one of the most daunting challenges faced by the Federal Government. With more 8-10 million illegal aliens already present in the United States and fewer than 2000 interior enforcement agents at its disposal, the Bureau of Immigration and Customs Enforcement (BICE) has a Herculean task on its hands-one that it simply cannot accomplish alone.

The assistance of state and local law enforcement agencies can mean the difference between success and failure in enforcing the immigration laws. The more than 650,000 police officers nationwide represent a massive force multiplier.

I will briefly summarize the legal authority upon which state and local police may currently act in rendering such assistance and then review relevant provisions of the proposed CLEAR Act. I will not cover the provisions of Section 287(g) of the Immigration and Nationality Act (INA), since the scope of such delegated authority is evident on the face of the act. Rather, I will discuss the inherent authority that has been possessed and exercised by state and local police since the earliest days of federal immigration law.

It has long been widely recognized that state and local police possess the inherent authority to arrest aliens who have violated *criminal* provisions of the INA. Once the arrest is made, the police officer must contact federal immigration authorities and transfer the alien into their custody within a reasonable period of time. Bear in mind that the power to arrest, and take temporary custody of, an immigration law violator is a subset of the broader power to "enforce." This is most salient distinction between inherent *arrest* authority and 287g authority to *enforce*-which includes arresting, investigating, preparing a case, and all of the other powers of the exercised by BICE agents.

Where some confusion has existed in recent years is on the question of whether the same authority extends to arresting aliens who have violated civil provisions of the INA that render an alien deportable. This confusion was, to some extent, fostered by an erroneous 1996 opinion of the Office of Legal Counsel (OLC) of the Department of Justice. That opinion, the relevant part of which has since been withdrawn by OLC, indicated that while states did possess the authority to arrest aliens for criminal violations of the INA, congressional preemption barred the states from arresting aliens for civil violations of the act. In 2002, OLC corrected this error, withdrew the relevant portion of the 1996 opinion on its website, and produced a new opinion which thoroughly analyzed the issue. Although the Attorney General did not publish the 2002 opinion, the Attorney General did announce OLC's unequivocal conclusion that arresting aliens who have violated either criminal provisions or civil provisions that render an alien deportable "is within the inherent authority of the states."

This conclusion has been confirmed by every court to squarely address the issue. Indeed, it is difficult to make a persuasive case to the contrary. That said, I will proceed to offer my opinion as to why this conclusion is correct.

THE INHERENT ARREST AUTHORITY POSSESSED BY STATES

The preliminary question is whether states have inherent power (subject to federal preemption) to make arrests for violation of federal law. That is, may state police, exercising state law authority only, make arrests for violation of federal law, or do they have power to make such arrests only insofar as they are exercising delegated federal executive power? The answer to this question is plainly the former.

The source of this authority flows from the States' status as sovereign entities. As Chief Justice Marshall explained, "it was neither necessary nor proper to define the powers retained by the States. These powers proceed, not from the people of America, but from the people of the several States; and remain, after the adoption of the constitution, what they were before, except so far as they may be abridged by that instrument." *Sturges v. Crowninshield*, 17 U.S. (4 Wheat.) 122, 193 (1819).

It is well established that the authority of state police to make arrests for violation of federal law is not limited to those instances in which they are exercising delegated federal power. Rather, such arrest authority inheres in the States' status as sovereign entities. It inheres in the ability of one sovereign to accommodate the interests of another sovereign. This is the same inherent authority that is exercised whenever a state law enforcement officer witnesses a federal crime being committed and makes an arrest. That officer is not acting pursuant to delegated federal power. Rather, he is exercising the inherent power of his state to assist another sovereign.

There is abundant case law on this point. No act of Congress has authorized state police to arrest for federal offenses when they act without an arrest warrant. Nonetheless, in *United States v. Di Re*, 332 U.S. 581 (1948), the Supreme Court, held that "in absence of an applicable federal statute the law of the state where an arrest without warrant takes place determines its validity," id. at 589, implicitly adopting the position that States have inherent authority to authorize their police to make warrantless arrests for federal criminal violations. See *id.* at 589-90. In *Miller v. United States*, the Court stated flatly that "in the . . . circumstance of an arrest for violation of federal law by state peace officers, . . . the lawfulness of the arrest without warrant is to be determined by reference to state law." 357 U.S. 301, 305 (1958) (citing *Di Re*, 332 U.S. 581, 589). Similarly, in *Marsh v. United States*, 29 F.2d 172 (2d Cir. 1928), Judge Learned Hand's opinion for the Second Circuit construed a New York statute to authorize state police to make warrantless arrests for violation of federal law. *Id.* at 174. In so doing, Judge Hand specifically rejected the argument that the existence of a federal statute governing state arrests pursuant to warrant for federal offenses should be understood to preempt state officers from making warrantless arrests for federal offenses: "it would be unreasonable to suppose that [the United States'] purpose was to deny to itself any help that the states may allow." *Id.* Judge Hand's analysis plainly started from the premise that states have inherent authority to make arrests for federal offenses. This authority exists unless the federal government has preempted it or state law otherwise constrains it.

The Ninth and Tenth Circuits have expressed this understanding specifically in the immigration context. In *Gonzales v. City of Peoria*, 722 F.2d 468 (9th Cir. 1983), the Ninth Circuit declared that the "general rule is that local police are not precluded from enforcing federal statutes," id. at 474, and engaged in a preemption analysis to assess whether Congress had precluded state police enforcement of the criminal provisions of federal immigration law. *See id.* The Tenth Circuit has similarly opined that a "state trooper has general investigatory authority to inquire into possible immigration violations," *United States v. Salinas-Calderon*, 728 F.2d 1298, 1301 n.3 (10th Cir. 1984), and has applied preemption analysis to determine whether a federal statute "limit[s] or displace[s] the preexisting general authority of state or local police officers to investigate and make arrests for violations of federal law, including immigration laws," *United States v. Vasquez-Alvarez*, 176 F.3d 1294, 1295 (10th Cir. 1999).

THE ABSENCE OF CONGRESSIONAL PREEMPTION

In conducting preemption analysis, courts must look for (1) express preemption by congressional statement, (2) field preemption where the federal regulatory scheme is so pervasive as to create the inference that Congress intended to leave no room for the states to supplement it, or (3) conflict preemption, where compliance with both state and federal law is impossible or state law prevents the accomplishment of congressional objectives. *See Gade v. National Solid Wastes Mgmt. Ass'n*, 505 U.S. 88, 98 (1992) (plurality opinion). In all three categories, there must exist manifest congressional intent for preemption to exist. With respect to immigration arrests, because there is no case of direct conflict, the only types of preemption that are even possible are field preemption and express preemption.

Moreover, in the context of state arrests for violations of federal law, there is a particularly strong presumption against preemption. Unlike the typical preemption scenario, a state arrest for a violation of federal law does not involve an attempt by states to enact state laws, or to promulgate regulations pursuant to state laws, that arguably conflict with federal law or intrude into a field that is reserved to Congress or that federal law has occupied. Rather, the question is whether states can assist the federal government by arresting aliens who have violated federal law and by turning them over to federal authorities. And the critical starting presumption must be that the federal government did not intend to deny itself any assistance that states might offer. *See* 29 F.2d at 174.

In 1996, Congress expressly put to rest any suspicion that it did not welcome state and local assistance in making immigration arrests. Congress added section 287(g) to the INA, providing for the establishment of written agreements with state law enforcement agencies to convey federal immigration enforcement functions to such agencies. In doing so, Congress reiterated its understanding that states and localities may make immigration arrests regardless of whether a 287(g) agreement exists. Congress stated that a formal agreement is *not necessary* for "any officer or employee of a State or political subdivision of a state . . . to communicate with the Attorney General regarding the immigration status of any individual, including reporting knowledge that a particular alien is not lawfully present in the United States," or "otherwise to cooperate with the Attorney General in the identification, apprehension, detention, or removal of aliens not lawfully present in the United States." 8 U.S.C. § 1357(g)(10).

Consequently, it is hardly surprising that no appellate court has expressly ruled that states are preempted from arresting aliens for civil violations of the INA. The only case that even comes close is the 1983 opinion of the Ninth Circuit in *Gonzales v. City of Peoria*, 722 F.2d 468 (9th Cir. 1983). In *Gonzales*, the Ninth Circuit held that local police officers have the authority to arrest an alien for a violation of the criminal provisions of the INA if such an arrest is authorized under state law. In that instance, a group of persons of Mexican descent challenged a policy of the City of Peoria, Arizona, that instructed local police to arrest and detain aliens suspected of illegally entering the United States in violation of the criminal prohibitions of section 1325 of title 8. *See* 722 F.2d at 472-73. Observing that local police generally are not precluded from enforcing federal statutes and that concurrent enforcement authority is authorized where local enforcement would not impair federal regulatory interests, the court engaged in a preemption analysis to determine whether Congress had precluded local enforcement of this criminal provision of the INA. The court concluded that no such preemption had occurred. *See id.* at 475. In passing, the Ninth Circuit "assume[d] that the civil provisions of the [INA] ... constitute . . . a pervasive regulatory scheme" that suggested a congressional intent to preempt local enforcement, *id.* at 474-75. However, this was possibility of field preemption merely an *assumption*, asserted without any analysis, and made in *dictum*-entirely outside of the holding of the case (which concerned a criminal offense). It does not constitute binding precedent. And even if the Ninth Circuit had squarely reached this conclusion in 1983, such a holding would have been fatally undermined by the court's failure to apply the strong presumption against preemption discussed above. Moreover, the actions of Congress in 1996 made such a holding unsustainable.

In contrast, the case law supporting the conclusion that Congress has *not* preempted state arrests of aliens for violations of civil provisions of the INA is solid and on point. The Tenth Circuit has issued several opinions on the subject, all pointing to the conclusion that Congress has never sought to preempt the states' inherent authority to make immigration arrests for both criminal and civil violations of the INA. Its 1984 ruling in the case of *United States v. Salinas-Calderon*, 728 F.2d 1298 (10th Cir. 1984), confirmed the inherent arrest authority possessed by the states. The defendant in that case was the driver of a pickup who had been arrested for the criminal violation of transporting illegal aliens. He had been stopped by a state trooper for driving erratically. The driver and his wife were in the cab; and six passengers, none of whom spoke English, were in the back of the pickup. The defendant claimed that a state trooper did not have the authority to detain the transported passengers while he questioned them about their immigration status. In rejecting this claim, the Tenth Circuit held that a "state trooper has general investigatory authority to inquire into possible immigration violations." 728 F.2d at 1301 n.3. The court did not differentiate between criminal and civil violations. Indeed, because there is no indication in the opinion that there was any reason to believe that the alien passengers had committed any criminal violations, the court's statement appears to apply fully to civil as well as criminal violations.

The Tenth Circuit's most salient case on the preemption question is *U.S. v. Vasquez-Alvarez*, 176 F.3d 1294 (10th Cir. 1999). In that case, an Oklahoma police officer arrested the defendant because he was an "illegal alien." The officer did not know at the time whether the defendant had committed a civil or criminal violation of the INA. *Id.* at 1295. It was later discovered that the alien had illegally reentered the country after deportation, in violation of 8 U.S.C. § 1326, a criminal violation. When the government indicted the defendant, he moved to suppress his post-arrest statements, fingerprints, and identity, arguing that he was arrested in violation of 8 U.S.C. § 1252c. The defendant claimed that a local police officers could arrest an illegal alien only in accordance with the restrictions set forth in section 1252c and that because his arrest was not carried out according that provision it was unauthorized. Section 1252c authorizes state and local police to make a warrantless arrest and to detain an illegal alien if (1) the arrest is permitted by state and local law, (2) the alien is illegally present in the United States, (3) the alien was previously convicted of a felony in the United States and subsequently was deported or left the country, and (4) prior to the arrest the police officer obtains appropriate confirmation of the alien's status from federal immigration authorities. 8 U.S.C. § 1252c.

The Tenth Circuit's conclusion was unequivocal: section 1252c "does not limit or displace the preexisting general authority of state or local police officers to investigate and make arrests for violations of federal law, including immigration laws. Instead, section 1252c merely creates an additional vehicle for the enforcement of federal immigration law." *Vasquez-Alvarez*, 176 F.3d at 1295. Citing its earlier decision in *Salinas-Calderon*, the court observed that it had "held that state law-enforcement officers have the general authority to investigate and make arrests for violations of federal immigration laws." *Vasquez-Alvarez*, 176 F.3d at 1296. The court rejected the alien's contention that all arrests not authorized by section 1252c are prohibited by it. The court found no congressional intent in the text of section 1252c to preempt existing state authority to enforce federal immigration laws. *See id.* at 1297-98. The court also opined that the legislative history of section 1252c supported its conclusion. Citing the comments of Representative Doolittle, the sponsor of the floor amendment that later became section 1252c, the court stated that "the purpose of § 1252c was to displace a perceived federal limitation on the ability of state and local officers to arrest aliens in the United States in violation of Federal immigration laws." *Id.* at 1298-99. However, the court noted that Representative Doolittle did not identify the source of this perceived limitation; neither the defendant nor the government had identified such a law; and the court itself had "not been able to identify any pre-§ 1252c limitations on the powers of state and local officers to enforce federal law." *Id.* at 1299 n.4. The court concluded that the "legislative history does not contain the slightest indication that Congress intended to displace any preexisting enforcement powers already in the hands of state and local officers." *Id.* at 1299. Finally, the court drew additional support for its conclusion from the fact that "in the months following the enactment of section 1252c, Congress passed a series of provisions designed to encourage cooperation between the federal government and the states in the enforcement of federal immigration laws." *Id.* at 1300 (citing 8 U.S.C. §§ 1103(a)(9), (c), 1357(g)).

Indeed, if section 1252c were somehow to be read to preempt state arrest authority, it would lead to an untenable reading of the law; the preemptive effect would have to extend to all state arrests for violations involving illegal presence in the United States. That is, state police would be able to arrest only those aliens who were convicted felons and who had thereafter left or been deported from the United States. Because such aliens are not readily identifiable visually, this would mean "that there is no means of securing offenders caught in flagrante"-as Judge Hand observed-"a result which would so impair the execution of the laws that it seems to us incredible it should have been intended." *Marsh*, 29 F.2d at 174. There is simply no evidence in the legislative history of section 1252c to support such a reading.

The Fifth Circuit has also rejected the notion that Congress has preempted the inherent arrest authority possessed by the states. In *Lynch v. Cannatella*, 810 F.2d 1363 (5th Cir. 1987), the court considered whether 8 U.S.C. §1223(a) defined the sole process for detaining alien stowaways, thereby preempting harbor police from detaining illegal aliens as occurred in that case. The Eighth Circuit's conclusion was broad and unequivocal: "No statute precludes other federal, state, or local law enforcement agencies from taking other action to enforce this nation's immigration laws." *Id.* at 1371.

Finally, on the subject of preemption, it must be noted that the distinction between arrests by state police for criminal violations of the INA and arrests for civil violations of the INA is utterly unsustainable. None of the statutes that have been considered by the courts under claims of express preemption contain such a distinction. And any claim of field preemption would have to establish that the civil provisions of the INA create a pervasive regulatory scheme indicating congressional intention to preempt, while the criminal provisions do not. The structure of the INA, with its numerous overlapping civil and criminal provisions, does not support such a distinction.

THE CLEAR ACT

Passage of H.R. 2671 is an important and step that must be taken if the voluntary cooperation of state and local police in the enforcement of immigration laws is to be maximized. And such cooperation is necessary if the rule of law is ever to be fully restored to immigration in this country. I do have several suggestions that may assist the committee in strengthening H.R. 2671. They are as follows.

<u>Section 101-Affirmation of Inherent Arrest Authority</u>. It is important that nothing in the CLEAR Act be misinterpreted by the Executive Branch or by the Judiciary as narrowing the inherent arrest authority that the states already possess. The current wording says that

"law enforcement personnel of a State . . . are *authorized*" to investigate and detain illegal aliens. I strongly recommend that the committee not use the word "authorized," because it implies that Congress is authorizing or conferring these arrest powers upon the states. That is, of course, unnecessary since the authority is already possessed by the states and it flows from their inherent powers as sovereign entities within our federalist system. What should be stated unequivocally is that Congress has never preempted this authority. Such a statement would prevent courts from making any mistake on this account. I would also note that the inherent authority does not extend to "removal," in the broad sense of adjudicating an alien's status and returning the alien to his country of origin. Therefore, I suggest the following alternative phrasing of Section 101:

"Notwithstanding any other provision of law, it is recognized that law enforcement personnel of a State or political subdivision of a State possess the inherent authority of sovereign governments to investigate, apprehend, detain, and transport aliens who are unlawfully present in the United States (including the transportation of such aliens across State lines to detention centers or to federal custody), in the enforcement of the immigration laws of the United States. It is further recognized that no Act of Congress has ever preempted this authority with respect to either criminal violations or civil violations of federal immigration law."

Section 103-Criminal Penalties and Forfeiture of Assets. With respect to this section, I wish to note at the outset that the Committee has correctly recognized that illegal immigration imposes a massive financial burden on all levels of government. The costs of providing education, health care, and other social services, combined with the law enforcement costs that are incurred regardless of whether a state chooses to cooperate in enforcing immigration laws, are staggering. The meager taxes collected from illegal aliens do not come close to reimbursing governments at the local, state, and federal level. It is estimated that the net cost of illegal immigration totals approximately $40 billion per year. The forfeiture of assets is an appropriate mechanism to allow governments to begin to recover these costs. It is also a substantial deterrent to those who would flaunt our immigration laws.

I would like to offer two minor suggestions to improve Section 103. First, it would be useful to create a blanket criminal misdemeanor offense that applies to any alien who violates any provision of U.S. immigration law or is unlawfully present in the United States. This would eliminate any ambiguity that persists regarding arrests for criminal versus civil violations of immigration law. It would also defeat the misinformation campaign that has been launched by organizations hostile to the enforcement of immigration laws. Second, I suggest that in Section 103(a), in the provision amending Section 275(b) of the Immigration and Nationality Act, after the phrase "after the expiration of a nonimmigrant visa" the following words should be inserted: "or after the end of the alien's period of authorized stay in the United States." This would cover those situations in which the alien's visa is valid for a period beyond the period for which the alien is actually authorized to stay in the United States. This is common with B(1) and B(2) visas that may be valid for as long as ten years, even though the alien has only been authorized to stay in the United States for a period of six months.

Section 104-Sharing of Information Through NCIC. This section is an extremely important component of the CLEAR Act. As the Committee is aware, the sharing of information with state and local law enforcement agencies through the National Criminal Information Center (NCIC) of the Department of Justice has improved substantially since the attacks of September 11, 2001. However, there are bureaucratic and institutional forces that have slowed the entry of information regarding aliens into the NCIC database. I suggest that the Committee reword Section 104 slightly, in order to (1) make the obligation to provide such information unmistakable and (2) to accelerate the entry of information regarding alien absconders. I suggest the following wording:

"Provision of Information to the NCIC.- Within 180 days after the date of the enactment of this section, the Under Secretary for Border and Transportation Security of the Department of Homeland Security shall provide the National Criminal Information Center of the Department of Justice with all information relevant for the apprehension of all persons who are known to have violated any immigration law of the United States. Thereafter, the Under Secretary shall be required to provide such information to the National Criminal Information Center with respect to each new violation that is discovered within 180 days after such violation becomes known to the Department of Homeland Security. The names and particulars of aliens who have disregarded or disobeyed a final order of removal shall be provided to the National Criminal Information Center regardless of whether the alien's failure to depart was willful and regardless of whether the alien received actual notice of the final order of removal."

The alien absconder problem is of such immense magnitude that it has made an utter mockery of the rule of law. There are now more than 400,000 absconders at large in the United States. These aliens have had their day in immigration court and have disobeyed a final order of removal. A substantial number of absconders have engaged in serious criminal activity in addition to their immigration violations. Most absconders have committed criminal violations of the INA. Others have committed civil violations only, if the underlying immigration violation was of a civil provision and the refusal to obey the order of removal was not willful. At the end of 2001, the Department of Justice and the INS launched the absconder initiative, which has continued under the Department of Homeland Security. Under this initiative, the process of listing absconders in the NCIC database was begun. Although the initiative has yielded many valuable arrests with the cooperation of state and local law enforcement, the effort has been hamstrung by the fact that the entry of names into the NCIC database has occurred at an alarmingly slow rate. Indeed, the number of absconders is growing faster than the entry of absconders into NCIC. A primary reason is for this slow rate of entry is the current practice of attempting to ascertain whether federal immigration officials effected actual notice of the final order of removal. This is, of course, difficult when the alien has changed address without informing the immigration court or when the alien has become a fugitive. The inherent legal authority of a state or local law enforcement officer to make the arrest exists regardless of whether notice was effected. Therefore, this unnecessary impediment to the rapid entry of absconder data into the NCIC system should be unequivocally removed.

Section 108-Claims by States and Localities Against the Federal Government. This section provides a useful incentive to ensure that the federal government remains a faithful partner in the cooperative effort to enforce immigration laws. I suggest only a minor clarification here. Section

108(a)(2), as currently drafted, indicates that the decisions of the administrative law judge "may be appealed only to the Attorney General or the Secretary of Homeland Security...." I would delete "or the Secretary of Homeland Security." Because Section 108 locates the administrative law judge within the Department of Justice, and because it is consistent with the adjudication of immigration law questions by the immigration courts of the Department of Justice, it is appropriate that the Attorney General review any appeals. Ambiguity as to the final arbiter of such cases would only exacerbate the sensitivity that will inevitably surround such cases.

New Section 114-The Issuance of Driver's Licenses to Illegal Aliens. As the Committee is no doubt aware, the issuance of driver's licenses to illegal aliens by some states jeopardizes immigration law enforcement, general law enforcement, and national security. The driver's license effectively serves as the basic identity document in America today. It is a de facto national identity card issued by more than 50 different jurisdictions. Driver's licenses allow illegal aliens to operate with ease in American society and escape the scrutiny that might otherwise occur in routine law enforcement encounters. On our northern border the driver's license operates as an effective substitute for a U.S. passport, allowing an alien who is persuasive in falsely asserting U.S. citizenship to cross the border freely.

Permitting illegal aliens to acquire driver's licenses also opens up opportunities for criminals, whether they be foreign nationals or U.S. citizens. States that allow illegal aliens to possess driver's licenses inevitably reduce the level of identity documentation that is required to obtain a license. The result is that criminals are able to use the lax standards to create false identities backed up by the imprimatur of a driver's license. Such false identities facilitate money laundering, credit card fraud, and check fraud. They also defeat the operation of the NCIC system, because criminals are able to evade arrest warrants by presenting fraudulently-obtained "clean" licenses during traffic encounters with local law enforcement officers. Worse, the driver's license becomes a useful tool in the hands of terrorists. Virginia issued licenses to eight of the 9/11 terrorists-licenses that likely were used to board the airplanes on that fateful day.

The most effective solution to this problem would be to make eligibility for federal highway funds contingent upon the states' denying driver's licenses to illegal aliens. Such funds should also be contingent upon states' setting expiration dates so that driver's licenses for legal aliens expire on the date that an alien's period of authorized stay terminates. The only documentation sufficient to qualify an alien for a driver's license should be a valid passport with a valid U.S. visa. This would allow state and local police officers to draw reasonable conclusions from an alien's possession of an unexpired driver's license.

In summary, it is clear that state and local police possess substantial inherent authority to make immigration arrests. It is also clear that the potential for closer cooperation with state and local law enforcement has not been fully exploited. Consequently, there has been a cost in the national security of the United States, as well as in the enforcement of immigration laws. The CLEAR Act would improve the situation substantially. I appreciate the efforts of this Committee to address these issues and the opportunity to share my perspective.

Courtesy of James R. Edwards Jr., The MITA Group

Appendix E

IMMIGRATION ENFORCEMENT RESOURCES FOR STATE/LOCAL LAW ENFORCEMENT

287(g) Program

Gives state and local law enforcement departments a way of obtaining in-depth immigration enforcement training, and Immigration and Customs Enforcement cooperation and resources for a number of their police officers. Requires a Memorandum of Agreement. The 287(g)-trained officers assist with immigration enforcement at the local or state level, including identification of immigration status of aliens in the custody of their agency.

Contact ICE Investigations Office: (202) 514-6120 or ICE Special Agent in Charge in nearest ICE regional office; Information Packets at www.ice.gov/exec/s287g/section287g_packet_request.asp

Basic Immigration Enforcement Training E-Learning Pilot Project

Cameron University in Lawton, Oklahoma, has developed a Justice Department-funded pilot project to provide 500 state and local law enforcement officers with basic training in immigration enforcement through a web-based e-learning platform. Participation in BIET is free to law officers and agencies, and the program is enrolling officers. The training, based on Homeland Security-provided material, focuses on types of immigration status and forms of alien identification. The program allows participating officers to review the courses, research associated materials, and consult the training website continually. The training website is hosted on the secure, encrypted Internet backbone that supports the Federal Law Enforcement Training Center's Distributed Learning Program.

Those interested in participating in the pilot project should contact: customer-service@dcmsnet.info. They should mention "Basic Immigration Enforcement Training" in the subject line, and provide the following information: Name, Organization, City, State, Zip, Work phone, E-mail address.

Law Enforcement Support Center

LESC is operated by the Homeland Security Department and is available to state and local law enforcement, correctional facilities, and courts for phone consultation 24 hours a day, 7 days a week. LESC helps police agencies determine the immigration status and wants/warrants status of suspected criminal and/or illegal aliens in custody locally. These are foreign-born suspects encountered in the course of daily law enforcement duty. The center assists with alien suspect assessment using more than 10 law enforcement and intelligence databases, including eight within Homeland Security.

Contact the Law Enforcement Support Center via the National Law Enforcement Telecommunications System (NLETS) at: LESC Computer Services Division, 188 Harvest Lane, Williston, Vermont 05495 or by phone at (802) 872-6050 or via the NLETS Administrative Message (AM) to VTINS07S0.

Institutional Removal Program/Criminal Alien Program

Homeland Security inherited IRP from the former Immigration and Naturalization Service. IRP/CAP, now operated by the DHS Office of Detention and Removal and the ICE Office of Investigations, assists correctional facilities, jails, and prisons in identifying criminal aliens. Early in their incarceration, deportable aliens are identified and these criminal aliens are placed concurrently in removal (deportation) proceedings. This allows completion of civil due process in immigration proceedings while the deportable alien serves time behind bars on criminal offenses. Upon completion of the sentence, aliens are not released, but custody is transferred to federal immigration authorities.

Contact the ICE Office of Detention and Removal's Director, Office of Detention and Removal Operations, 801 I St., N.W., Suite 900, Washington, DC 20536 or by phone at (202) 305-2734. For more information or to locate the appropriate field office, see www.ice.gov.

Courtesy of James R. Edwards Jr., Olive, Edwards, & Cooper

ASPATORE

ASPATORE

www.Aspatore.com

Aspatore Books, a Thomson Reuters business, is the largest and most exclusive publisher of C-level executives (CEO, CFO, CTO, CMO, partner) from the world's most respected companies and law firms. Aspatore annually publishes a select group of C-level executives from the Global 1,000, top 250 law firms (partners and chairs), and other leading companies of all sizes. C-Level Business Intelligence™, as conceptualized and developed by Aspatore Books, provides professionals of all levels with proven business intelligence from industry insiders—direct and unfiltered insight from those who know it best—as opposed to third-party accounts offered by unknown authors and analysts. Aspatore Books is committed to publishing an innovative line of business and legal books, those which lay forth principles and offer insights that, when employed, can have a direct financial impact on the reader's business objectives, whatever they may be. In essence, Aspatore publishes critical tools—need-to-read as opposed to nice-to-read books—for all business professionals.

Inside the Minds

The critically acclaimed *Inside the Minds* series provides readers of all levels with proven business intelligence from C-level executives (CEO, CFO, CTO, CMO, partner) from the world's most respected companies. Each chapter is comparable to a white paper or essay and is a future-oriented look at where an industry/profession/topic is heading and the most important issues for future success. Each author has been selected based upon their experience and C-level standing within the professional community. *Inside the Minds* was conceived in order to give readers actual insights into the leading minds of business executives worldwide. Because so few books or other publications are actually written by executives in industry, *Inside the Minds* presents an unprecedented look at various industries and professions never before available.

Praise for *Inside the Minds*

"Need-to-read inside information and analysis that will improve your bottom line - the best source in the business." – Daniel J. Moore, Member, Harris Beach LLP

"The Inside the Minds series is a valuable probe into the thought, perspectives, and techniques of accomplished professionals…" – Chuck Birenbaum, Partner, Thelen Reid & Priest

"Aspatore has tapped into a gold mine of knowledge and expertise ignored by other publishing houses." – Jack Barsky, Managing Director, Information Technology & Chief Information Officer, ConEdison *Solutions*

"Unlike any other publisher – actual authors that are on the front-lines of what is happening in industry." – Paul A. Sellers, Executive Director, National Sales, Fleet and Remarketing, Hyundai Motor America

"A snapshot of everything you need..." – Charles Koob, Co-Head of Litigation Department, Simpson Thacher & Bartlet

"Everything good books should be - honest, informative, inspiring, and incredibly well-written." – Patti D. Hill, President, BlabberMouth PR

"Great information for both novices and experts." – Patrick Ennis, Partner, ARCH Venture Partners

"A rare peek behind the curtains and into the minds of the industry's best." – Brandon Baum, Partner, Cooley Godward

"Intensely personal, practical advice from seasoned dealmakers." – Mary Ann Jorgenson, Coordinator of Business Practice Area, Squire, Sanders & Dempsey

"Great practical advice and thoughtful insights." – Mark Gruhin, Partner, Schmeltzer, Aptaker & Shepard, PC

"Reading about real-world strategies from real working people beats the typical business book hands down." - Andrew Ceccon, Chief Marketing Officer, OnlineBenefits Inc.

"Books of this publisher are syntheses of actual experiences of real-life, hands-on, front-line leaders--no academic or theoretical nonsense here. Comprehensive, tightly organized, yet nonetheless motivational!" - Lac V. Tran, Sr. Vice President, CIO and Associate Dean Rush University Medical Center

"Aspatore is unlike other publishers…books feature cutting-edge information provided by top executives working on the front-line of an industry." - Debra Reisenthel, President and CEO, Novasys Medical Inc